Atomic Renaissance:
Women Mystery Writers of the 1940s and 1950s

D1447503

Titles by Jeffrey Marks

Canine Crimes
Canine Christmas
Magnolias and Mayhem
Who Was That Lady?
Craig Rice: The Queen of Screwball Mystery
The Ambush of My Name (A US Grant mystery)
Intent to Sell: Marketing the Genre Novel
A Good Soldier (A US Grant mystery)

Coming Soon:
Criminal Appetites
The Scent of Murder
Some Hidden Thunder (A US Grant mystery)

Atomic Renaissance:

Women Mystery Writers of the 1940s and 1950s

JEFFREY MARKS

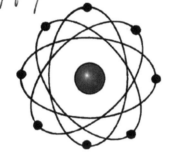

Delphi Books

Lee's Summit, MO

Delphi Books
PO Box 6435
Lee's Summit, MO 64064
DelphiBks@aol.com

Quantity discounts are available on bulk purchase of this book.

Publisher's Cataloging-in-Publication
(Provided by Quality Books, Inc.)

Marks, Jeffrey Alan, 1960-
    Atomic renaissance: women mystery writers of the 1940s and 1950 / Jeffrey Marks.
    p. cm.
    Includes bibliographical references and index.
    ISBN 0-9663397-7-0

    1. Detective and mystery stories, American Authorship. 2. American fiction -- Women authors. 3. Women--Ficiton I. Title

PN3448.D4M37 2003   813'.087089287
                         QBI33-1225

Library of Congress Catalog Number: 2003093155
First Delphi Books Printing: September 2003
Manufactured in the United States
10 9 8 7 6 5 4 3 2 1

To Tony
For his love and support

Acknowledgements

This book began as a tribute to all the wonderful writers I encountered while working on Craig Rice's biography. Too many women did not have their lives appropriately documented. To the people who have kept the details of these lives alive, I want to say thanks for the assistance. The amount of help I have received in writing this book has been legion. If I have left out a name, it is not from a lack of appreciation; it's only my faulty memory.

I can never sing the praises of our public library system loud enough. Oh that we could divert our defense budget to these worthwhile people for one year! The Glendale, California Library System sent me pages of information on Charlotte Armstrong and aided me with all the research on her life. J. Alec West put me in touch with them, and I owe him a huge debt of gratitude.

No acknowledgement list would be complete without thanking the university library system as well. Boston University Library has a wonderful collection of mystery authors' correspondence. Nathaniel Parks has been incredible, helping me with virtually every author that I chose to profile. Additionally, Lilly Library at Indiana University is always a joy to work with. The Boucher / White collection never fails to amaze me with its breadth and depth. Thanks too to the Maryland Historical Society for its help with the Leslie Ford transcripts and to the University of New Mexico and Rose Diaz for their help with the Dorothy B. Hughes transcripts.

To the families of the authors, thank you as well for opening your families and memories to me. I appreciate the efforts of the Lewi family who wrote a wonderful memoir of their life with their mother.

The flanx of editors who read my book, made comments and helped were invaluable to me. Hats off to Rob Perry for his comments, to Rob Day for making me laugh as he used all my red pens on my book. Dean James answered millions of my questions patiently and politely as a good Southern gentleman would. I definitely want to thank all three of them.

Christina Albin Laboski did a wonderful job on the cover, and helped with the images in the book. It's not easy to be brilliant and pregnant at the same time, but somehow she managed.

My own family has been incredibly gracious about accepting my writing into our family when these women occupied so much of my thought. Other families might have thought me crazy for spending so much time locked in the past. Mine accepted my mania and helped to talk about it as I could. My parents have always loved and accepted me for who I am, for that I am eternally and perpetually grateful. My sister is a rock of support in designer clothes, and her two boys will talk for hours with me about ideas for more books and more book parties. Of course, Tony listens to me and manages while I have my nose stuck in a book. All these people mean a lot to me.

Table of Contents

Introduction

The world order convulsed in 1945 and the mystery genre shook with it. No realm was exempt from the societal changes following the end of World War II and radical changes in the writing of the detective mysteries ensued.

The first Golden Age of mystery had ended with the advent of the Second World War. This pinnacle in mystery fiction is usually defined as the time between the great wars, 1918 to 1939. During this era, the Great Detective ruled, a larger-than-life character whose deductive brain solved the vital puzzle.

While England boasted many women authors during the first Golden Age, the U.S. could not. Only a few American women wrote detective stories on our soil prior to World War II. Anna Katherine Green, recognized as one of the earliest female mystery authors with *The Leavenworth Case* in 1878, didn't publish much beyond the start of World War I. Her detectives were archetypal busybodies, nosy single women like Amelia Butterworth and Violet Strange.

One of the few American woman authors of the first Golden

Age, Mary Roberts Rinehart, established a firm place in the hearts of her fans during the first three decades of the 1900s. She wrote romantic suspense, now frequently derided as gothic or the "Had I But Known" school of mystery. Her books featured heroines who foolishly plunged into the danger of an isolated basement or darkened hallway, saying afterwards "Had I but known what murderous villain waited for me." Her novels paved the way for mysteries with more romantic interest, such as those written by Mignon G. Eberhart and Leslie Ford.

Another American woman, Carolyn Wells, began her own mystery series in 1909, featuring Fleming Stone. The sixty-one book series spanned four decades and covered a period in American history that included women's suffrage, flappers, and later, working women.

During the long years of the Second World War, the traditional mystery lost popularity. American men who had fought in Europe and the Pacific no longer cared for cozy, estate home murders. They had seen war and death in reality. Their new fiction had to reflect the darker, harder life the soldiers had seen in Europe and the Pacific. The frightening thought of other countries unleashing nuclear bombs invaded the veterans' fiction as well.

By 1945, the middle class returned to the U.S. greeted by rising incomes and unprecedented demand for consumer goods. After sixteen years of depression and then rations, American buyers wanted new and improved everything, including fiction.

Adding to the changes in the genre, many of the more blithe puzzle practitioners passed away before the end of the war or pursued other interests. Leaders in the field, like S. S. Van Dine, had passed away before Pearl Harbor. Others, like Ellery Queen, changed roles in the genre following the war, concentrating more on the publication of literary criticism and his magazine. The loss of these American authors left the gentler side of the genre near empty by the end of the war.

Yet even with these losses, English mystery writing changed little after 1945. Agatha Christie continued to publish a book or two per year. Some of her best work came from the late 1940s and early 1950s: *The Hollow, A Murder is Announced,* and *Funerals are Fatal* among them. The form was safe in England with its Grand Dame at the helm. Even today, many reviewers and bookstores classify the "British Cozy" as a subgenre in mystery.

However, America had changed, becoming more concerned with the nuclear horrors unleashed in 1945. The Cold War and McCarthyism brought a new type of mystery category to life, the spy novel. The fears of Communist takeover led to a new fiction category replacing the deduction of a crafty killer with the hunt for a mysterious agitator who threatened the world and "our way of life". This type of book was almost exclusively masculine in nature; the spy was a "super man" who loved women and lots of them. His hyper-masculinity meshed well with the gritty private eye novels being written by Mickey Spillane and similar authors. This new fiction left little room for women authors at a time when more women were writing mysteries.

More traditional mysteries still could be found in shorter formats. The popularity of digest-sized collections of short stories made for an easier way to read mystery fiction. The writers and characters who survived the changes in the mystery form now found their names in these short story magazines. Ellery Queen, Craig Rice, The Saint, Mickey Spillane, and Ed McBain had magazines named after them, which provided new mystery outlets. The television program *Alfred Hitchcock Presents* became a fertile ground for mystery short stories; Hitchcock used short mystery fiction for many of his half-hour television episodes. Author Charlotte Armstrong wrote for his series in 1960.

After a short flirtation with short stories in the 1950s, publishers winnowed the magazines to three or four. With that reduction in magazines, the genre was considered to be heading into decline. Some critics even declared the traditional mystery novel dead, replaced by spy fiction and private eyes.

Geo-political factors were not the only cause of change in the reading habits of Americans. Television became a national pastime with ownership rising dramatically during the 1950s. Public consumption of books suffered with the fascination for this new medium. The reliance on technology and science to cure all ills led to a decrease in the use of the written word to communicate ideas. Why envision an imaginary place of words when an entire galaxy of images beckoned? The changes of the era hurt sales of the writers, but gave them a freedom to try new techniques and to fail as well.

While the channels available in mystery fiction had shrunk, the number of women who wrote grew. In the years from 1945 through 1960, an element of experimentation in American detective fiction flourished, especially among women authors who found themselves excluded from the private eye and spy fiction establishments. These women authors took the crime novel in new and innovative directions since the prevailing forms had so little use for them. They wrote about places not usually mentioned in fiction, about psychological traumas unheard of outside of textbooks and non-traditional protagonists.

The women in this book are authors who staked a place in mystery fiction and moved the genre forward into its rebirth. Their creativity and talent marked them as unique in this era and as touchstones for writers to come. Tragically, their influences on later authors are almost all that remains. Most of the authors who wrote in this period are no longer in print today, despite being exceptional writers.

This generation of authors, even though their ages vary by about a decade and a half, would be the first to have unheralded opportunities available to them. They lived on the cusp of great changes in our society: air travel, birth control, greater civil rights. Women discovered the inventions that would free them from the hard work of the kitchens and family. New choices abounded. They could have family, home, career, and adventure.

Nonetheless, the seven authors whose biographies appear in *Atomic Renaissance* were hampered by their family obligations in ways that men were not. Even burdened by these additional duties, these women created the architecture for the second Golden Age of mystery, the rebirth of all types of mystery fiction that started in the 1980s. The selected authors include top sellers, Mystery Writers of America (MWA) presidents, Edgar award winners, and MWA Grand Masters. They contributed to the films of the day, both as scriptwriters and sources. Without these seven women, today's form would be severely narrowed in scope. The subgenres we know as regionals, gay and lesbian, strong women detectives, psychological suspense, softboiled suspense novels, and historical mysteries had their beginnings with these authors.

All of these writers worked in the period between mystery's Golden Ages, in a time where most male crime writers wrote about men fighting men. That is not to say that all these women wrote identically. All seven women took the design of the great detective and made it their own. Patricia Highsmith's stories of guilt and redemption can only be superficially compared to the psychological insights of Margaret Millar or the layered dark suspense yarns of Dorothy B. Hughes. Even though each author is different, every one of these seven took the crime novel in a different direction at a time where its future was uncertain. By the use of non-traditional characters and places, the novels expanded the definition of crime fiction. Indeed, Charlotte Armstrong's Edgar award-winning *A Dram of Poison* didn't even include a death in the book, a concept unlikely a generation before.

Their styles ranged from bleak to hysterical. Phoebe Atwood Taylor had a style unlike any other mystery author then or now. Whether writing about stern Asey Mayo or comical Leonidas Witherall, her humor and the strong regional flavor of her books are evident.

These seven authors helped pave the way for Marcia Muller's Sharon McCone, who in turn helped open the door for Sara Paretsky's V. I. Warshawski and Sue Grafton's Kinsey Millhone. The authors behind these characters helped to bring Sisters-in-Crime to life and make the playing field in the genre more level. The male-dominated mystery world of the 1950s could never have predicted the changes to the form.

This is not to say these seven are the only writers who affected the genre during this time period. Other authors, both well-known and popular, wrote during the 1940s and 1950s. Mary Roberts Rinehart and Craig Rice are not included here because their works do not change and grow to the same extent that these seven authors do. Other authors like Helen McCloy, Helen MacInnes, and Celia Fremlin, through their life events and the volume of their works, deserve full-length biographies to explore their contributions to mystery.

Additionally, a number of authors deserve more recognition than they currently receive: Dorothy Salisbury Davis; Kelley Roos who wrote the delightful Jeff and Haila Troy series; Frances Crane who wrote a series with colorful titles that preceded John D. MacDonald by over a decade: Hannah Lees; Mildred Davis who had a talent for edge of the seat thrillers; and many more.

There were other authors who made a huge splash in their time, but have faded without a ripple. This collection of authors had a lasting impact on the genre through their innovations to the crime novel of the 1940s and 1950s. Their history has helped to determine our present in the mystery field.

CHAPTER 1 — Margaret Millar

Margaret Millar is more readily recognized as Mrs. Ross Macdonald today than as an exceptional mystery author in her own right. Yet in the decades following World War II, Millar won numerous honors for her novels. She garnered three nominations for the Best Novel Edgar, the award for writing excellence from the Mystery Writers of America (MWA). In 1956, she won for *Beast in View,* a highly original work based on the then-newly posited multiple-personality disorder that has been frequently imitated in recent years. She served as president of the MWA the year following her Edgar win. In 1983 she received MWA's Grand Master Award for continued excellence in mystery writing. When Ross Macdonald served as MWA President decades after his wife, he admitted to playing catch-up. "I've aspired to [the MWA presidency], the more intensely in the years since Margaret Millar was elected President of MWA."[1] The

---

1. Matthew Bruccoli. *Ross MacDonald* (San Diego, CA: Hart Brace Janovich, 1984). page 86.

couple remains the only married pair to both serve as MWA presidents and receive Grand Master awards.

Millar's work was better recognized than her husband's writing until the early 1970s when Paul Newman starred in *Harper* and *The Drowning Pool* based on Macdonald's work. Yet her less-prolific husband has been the subject of multiple biographies while Millar has fallen into relative obscurity. Most of her books are out of print today.

Born Margaret Ellis Sturm on February 5th, 1915, she grew up in Kitchner, Ontario, an hour outside of Toronto. Nothing in her early years suggested the source of her tense, uneasy mysteries of character. Her father served as mayor of Kitchner while she enjoyed the associated popularity. She was top of her class at Kitchner-Waterloo Collegiate Institute where she studied music. At the Institute, she made a passing acquaintance with Kenneth Millar, a quiet student shuttled between female relatives following his parents' divorce. Margaret and Ken participated on the debate team together and shared a literary bond by debuting in the same issue of the *KCI Grumbler*, the school's literary magazine. Margaret's story dealt with the fate of a dying pianist in Spain, while Ken's piece was a parody. Their early interactions appeared to have made little impact on the pair, as they barely remembered each other from KCI.

Sturm graduated from Kitchner-Waterloo Collegiate Institute and chose to attend the University of Toronto, majoring in classical scholarship. She ran into Millar again at the university's library (she was reading Thucydides in the original Greek). He was smitten with her. Once he got the courage to talk to her, the pair began dating. They married the day after Ken graduated. Margaret didn't complete college, choosing to drop out to further Ken's career. After honeymooning in Ann Arbor, the Millars returned to Canada. Ken attended the University of Toronto, in preparation for teaching high school English.

In 1939, the Millars had their only child, Linda. After being ordered to bed following the birth of their daughter, Margaret spent two weeks reading mysteries. Most female crime authors of the era wrote in the domestic tradition, the "body in the library" genre. Despite her earlier attempts at literature, Margaret hadn't been planning to write any more. However, the mysteries encouraged Margaret's desire to write a novel. Ken encouraged her by serving as first reader and editor.

Millar began writing humorous mysteries featuring private investigator Paul Prye. These early works did not foreshadow the dark tones of her later books. As with most mystery authors between the Golden Ages, she and her writing matured and changed with the times.

Doubleday published her first novel, *The Invisible Worm*, in 1941. More novels quickly followed. By 1943, Ken quit his teaching job in Kitchner, based on Margaret's writing income. He accepted an academic fellowship from the University of Michigan in Ann Arbor and the family moved to the United States. Since Ken had been born in the U.S., he had citizenship, which allowed the young family to travel between the two countries easily.

Similar to many of the authors between the Golden Ages, Millar's work can be divided into phases that allowed her continued publication. Her early work is lighter and humorous, with an emphasis on the foibles of her characters. She branched out to write non-mysteries following this phase, novels that pulled from her own childhood and that of her young daughter.

After her transitional period with forays into literary fiction, Millar wrote her most thought-provoking work: edgy, suspenseful works of character and the world of psychology. The humor still manifested itself in wry situations and minor characters, but the emphasis shifted to the fate of the characters caught in a situation beyond their control. Her protagonists possessed personality flaws that led to the dismal situations they found themselves trapped in, a situation that led up to the inevitable denouement sprung on the reader in the last words of the book. The protagonists' reactions to these circumstances became paramount.

When Ken entered the mystery genre after his wife, people assumed Margaret had influenced his writing along with his knowledge of mystery-writing techniques. In fact, he'd been writing nearly as long as his wife had. Critics and the public recognized her work earlier, while her husband's fame took longer to develop. By the time that Ken Millar began writing private eye novels, Margaret had already become a name in the field. In order to avoid the appearance of capitalizing on her name, he opted to use a pen name, Ross Macdonald, to avoid confusion.

Living in Ann Arbor, Ken and Margaret continued to write. The family befriended W. H. Auden, who had recently moved to Michigan from Brooklyn. In New York, Auden had lived in a house with other writers including stripper-turned-author Gypsy Rose Lee, who was finishing her first novel, *The G-String Murders*. Lee's book became a best-seller, securing Auden's lifelong interest in the genre. Auden was already a fan of Margaret's mysteries when Ken enrolled in one of Auden's graduate classes at the University of Michigan.

Later Ken would remember Auden fondly. "Both Margaret and I were writing mysteries at the time. He [Auden] was most encouraging to us. That kind of push is unbelievably important to a young writer. It gave us a push in the direction we were going anyway. It just couldn't have been equaled in any other way."[2]

Auden offered to put Ken in contact with his agency, New York Associates, but Ken Millar felt that Auden's well-known homosexuality might impede his career. Like many in that paranoid era, Ken worried about being labeled a deviant and shunned by New York

---

2. Gene Davidson and John Knoerle, "Ross MacDonald Interview", *Mystery*, (Nov./ Dec., 1979): page 8.

publishing (which didn't seem to affect Auden, oddly enough). Ironically, Ken's first published work, *The Dark Tunnel*, featured a transvestite as a major character.

Millar accepted her husband's decision on the matter of agents. Ken used Margaret's literary agency, Harold Ober Associates, to submit his early works. The family connection didn't provide much help. Margaret's publisher, Random House, wouldn't buy Ken's manuscripts because they didn't feel that a husband and wife should be writing for the same publishing house.

A marriage of two authors in the same genre is rather unusual. A household of mystery writers sparks comparisons. Faye and Jonathan Kellerman are one couple who both write best-selling mysteries. Another pair are author Marcia Muller and private eye writer Bill Pronzini. In the latter case, the likeness is interesting because the introduction of the Sharon McCone character by Muller in *Edwin of the Iron Shoes* is typically hailed as one of the markers of the second Golden Age and birth of the female private eye novels. Says Muller, "Actually, I think there are more advantages to it [a marriage of two mystery writers] than disadvantages because you're with someone who understands if you have a crazy schedule or problems that are specific to the writing field."[3] Ken and Margaret felt the same way, critiquing each other's works and working on technique together.

The Millars' work had little in common, down to their writing habits. Margaret was a morning writer. Ken wrote exclusively in the afternoon. They worked in different parts of the house so as not to disturb each other or to fight over shared resources. Still they did help each other as needed. Ken served as editor and first reader with most of Margaret's work and Margaret once told an interviewer that she taught Ken how to write dialogue so all the characters didn't speak

---

3. "Interview with Bill Pronzini and Marcia Muller" *Mystery Scene*, (Issue number 42): page. 18.

like Ken.

Attempts to spur spousal rivalry failed. Questioned about who was the better writer, Ken Millar said, "I honestly believe that she's the best in the business."[4] Despite the lack of competition, Ken's writing worried his wife. Margaret was concerned with the bleak, hard-boiled content of his work. As Ross Macdonald, her husband's oeuvre focused on variations on the theme of abandoned children and past crimes. The works were assumed to be autobiographical in nature. Dredging up his unhappy past took a toll on Macdonald's psyche. His moods grew dark as he wrote about his disjointed childhood.

Her husband's past concerned Margaret. Ken Millar never recovered from the pain of being abandoned by his father and shuttled between households populated mostly by women. He idolized his father, John, whose name he used as a pseudonym for some of his works. His father had played only a minor part in Ken's life. Yet in interviews and articles, Millar recounts numerous stories of his long-absent father and few of his mother. His works reflect that pain of separation and through his frequent use of orphans or lost souls in his writing.

Additionally, the years he spent traveling between relatives were shrouded in mystery. Millar hinted that he might have inadvertently seen murders at these temporary homes. He often referred to physical and emotional abuse as well as crimes he might have witnessed during this extended "foster" limbo. During these years, he drank, fought constantly, and experimented sexually with other men. While his past proved wonderful grist for his writing, it took a toll on his wife. As she wrote more, the edginess began to show in her work. The novels began to touch on emotional family issues as her books

---

4. Burt Prelutsky, "Big Fish in a Big Pond", *Los Angeles Times Calendar*, (November 25, 1973): page 18.

carried traces of Margaret's own home life. Margaret frequently used children as protagonists. Many of her books contained elements of hidden agendas inside a marriage.

Both authors used past crimes and relationships of characters as an impact on the crimes and mysteries of the present day. Even so, Millar states in the introduction to one of her works that given the same germ of an idea, she and Ross would take radically different approaches with the notion. Her books took place across the country, using familiar locales where she had lived. As Ross Macdonald, Ken wrote about Southern California. Her books were more psychological suspense; his were hard-boiled Lew Archer.

Millar's work is characterized by protagonists unique to the individual books she wrote. Even the tone of her books changed radically from terrifying to light-hearted. The circumstances of her life tainted what she wrote. Her themes range from mental illness to capers in which characters fight for an inheritance. She allowed the details of her personal life to appear in a more generalized family-in-jeopardy theme. Her main characters were often unmarried women raising families.

The length of her works stayed the same even though her characters changed radically. She wrote novels almost exclusively, preferring the in-depth portrait of her characters allowed by the longer form. The exception was a handful of short stories written for her friend and colleague, Fred Dannay (for *Ellery Queen's Mystery Magazine*).

Millar's work features amateur detectives, lawyers, and psychologists, rather than professional investigators. Until late in her career, she intentionally avoided using a private eye. When she finally experimented with the private eye novel, a hue and cry came over the mystery world along with the inevitable comparisons between protagonists. The experience only strengthened her resolve to stay away from the subgenre.

While critics recognized Macdonald as a literate author of crime novels and one of the more influential authors of his era, even his most ardent admirers admit that he wrote the same novel repeatedly. The Freudian Oedipal myth and his own unhappy childhood provided the impetus for his works including *The Galton Case*. On the other hand, Millar took a fancy to numerous different ideas around the complexity of the human mind. In most instances, the psychology and circumstances differed greatly. The author of the light-hearted *Rose's Last Summer* seems hardly capable of dark books like *The Fiend*, which deals with child abusers.

Many people wondered about the couple's relationship since most of Macdonald's books feature strong, determined women cast as either murderer or victim. There are no happy marriages in his books, and Millar wrote about a number of bleak couples in her work as well. The Millars could be contentious; both of them used their spouse in their books as unattractive characters. The pair had acrimonious battles in the early years of their life together. Regardless of the tone of their fictional families, the Millars' marriage mellowed into a happy one in their later years.

Happiness didn't equate to financial success. Their growing literary accolades didn't afford them a comfortable income. The earnings of two writers, even a couple as well known as the Millars, required a frugal lifestyle. During their best years, the couple's advances and royalties hardly topped twelve to fifteen thousand dollars a year. They did not have major financial success until Ken's novels were optioned by Hollywood. The pair didn't make a sufficient income together to purchase a house until 1965, after almost thirty years of marriage.

Even as Ken started to rehash his past in print, Margaret continued to evolve as a writer. Following three humorous mystery novels about a somewhat whimsical psychiatric detective named Paul Prye, Margaret Millar decided to put psychiatry to more serious uses.

She took Inspector Sands of the Toronto Police Department, a major secondary character in the final Prye novel, *The Devil Loves Me*, and made him her lead detective in *Wall of Eyes*. By 1945 with the second Sands novel, *The Iron Gates*, Margaret attracted the critical acclaim she deserved. The bizarre plot elements — a severed finger, an escape from a mental institution — complemented a solid psychological puzzle that kept the reader guessing until the final pages, trademarks of her best works. Since Millar opted not to use a recurring series character, these are the only novels about lonely, rather drab Inspector Sands. The reader encounters him a decade after the novels in a rare short story, "The Couple Next Door" which was published by Fred Dannay in *Ellery Queen's Mystery Magazine*.

As the war years progressed, the Millars moved to California from Michigan, following the pattern of her husband's nomadic past. After a short time out west, Ken Millar enlisted and served as an ensign in the Naval Reserves. He left his family alone with few friends on the West Coast. To support herself and her daughter, Margaret found work as a screenwriter. In 1945, she wrote the screenplay for *The Iron Gates*, an adaptation of her novel of the same name for Warner Brothers. The sale allowed Ken quit his teaching job when he returned from the service. He decided to pursue a full-time career as a mystery novelist.

Margaret briefly left mystery to try childhood memoirs. In Ken's absence along with an easing of his private demons, she turned to the subject of her own happy childhood. In *It's All in the Family*, Millar writes the episodic adventures of Priscilla, a young girl trying to come to grips with impending womanhood. Even though there's no mystery in the book, Millar's style still exudes suspense, a feeling that something momentous will happen. The character of a young girl, while no doubt modeled on her daughter, foreshadows the children who will show up in her later works.

After 1950, Millar took to mysteries exclusively. With the

exception of one nonfiction work (*The Birds and the Beasts Were Here*), she would never leave the genre again. Having written three non-mystery novels (*Experiment in Springtime, It's All in the Family, The Cannibal Heart*), Millar wrote mysteries of a different kind than she had before the war. Gone were the funny mysteries. She now concentrated on the suspense field, which was only found in small traces in her early works.

There's every indication that Millar was aware of the upheavals in the genre. Ken Millar noted, "developments in the American mystery field have been equally various and interesting." By 1941, Howard Haycraft had already noticed the abandonment of "rigid formulas in favor of blending the detective elements with the novel of manners and character." The realistic vein opened up by the *Black Mask* writers was enriched by the influence of classical literature and modern psychoanalysis. As her husband later noted, "Some of the most original and elegant work to come out of this new meld was penned by Margaret Millar."[5] Despite the obvious bias, it's evident that the Millars saw the changes in the mystery coming.

In the first Golden Age, psychological suspense and mysteries involving psychiatry didn't exist. Freud had proposed most of his theories of human behavior in the past three decades and Jung had only written about archetypes in 1921. Mystery writers used the well-worn character types and left the studies of personality to other novels. If anything, crime novels dealt with issues of class and morality.

After World War II, the changes in the American psyche didn't allow authors to return to the puzzle novels. The hardboiled school of mysteries, which had been introduced in the Great Depression, had appeared after the war with even more bleak pictures of humanity accompanied by heavy doses of gunplay and the personal

---

5. Ross Macdonald, *Self-Portrait: Ceaselessly into the Past* (San Bernadino, CA: Brownstone Mystery Guides, 1981). page 102.

ethics of the detective. A solid knowledge of real people, the middle and lower classes, was essential to this world-view.

On film, Hitchcock became one of the first to use psychologists in the late 1940s with his thriller, *Spellbound.* While characterization has always demanded an understanding of the human mind, the director was one of the first to use the theories of Freud and Jung openly in his work. In the movie, Gregory Peck stars as a man haunted by dreams and visions of a crime he can't comprehend. Salvador Dali helped Hitchcock with the surrealistic dream images for the movie. A psychiatrist treats Peck in order to get to the solution of the mystery.

Indeed, *Do Evil in Return* references the movie, *Spellbound.*

> "'I never saw a lady doctor so close up before. In the movies I have, though. Ingrid Bergman was a doctor in a movie once, fell in love with Gregory Peck, only Gregory Peck happened to be —.'
>
> "'Yes, I know. 'Spellbound.'''
>
> "'Yes, yes, That was it, 'Spellbound.' I don't know what she saw in Gregory Peck. He's skinny as a broom, besides being a nut—in the picture, I mean.'"[6]

The trend toward psychology continues to grow as a number of contemporary authors use psychology in their work. The current renaissance focuses more on character and motivation. Since publisher-demanded series characters are standard these days, the mystery novels need strong elements of character psychology in order to stay fresh. In addition, more and more psychologists and mental health workers are featured as amateur detectives.

6. Margaret Millar, *Do Evil in Return*, (New York: Random House, 1950). page 111.

Do Evil in Return features the story of Dr. Charlotte Keating, who is having an affair with the very-married Lewis Ballard, while she treats Lewis' wife for panic attacks. When a stranger comes in to Dr. Keating's office looking to end a pregnancy, Keating refuses to help. The doctor later regrets her decision not to help and seeks out the girl, who has disappeared. The disappearance leads to three more deaths before Keating realizes that the killings began much closer to home. Interestingly, the title is a quote from W. H. Auden, the Millars' friend.

Millar followed *Do Evil in Return* with the humorous *Rose's Last Summer* in 1952. Unfortunately, the book seems to be something of an experiment for Millar, an attempt to meld the suspense of her later works with the humor of her earlier efforts. The title character is a washed-up actress who disappears and turns up dead in a stranger's garden. Her friends and family turn to detecting to uncover the cause of her death and why she passed away so far from home. The police label her death as natural causes, but the tone of the book lets the reader know that there is more to this case than meets the eye.

The edgy quality of Millar's writing, the aura of dread which makes the reader turn the pages, didn't mesh well with slapstick. Traces of this taut quality exist in scenes like the one where Rose calls the social worker from beyond the grave, but its impact is minimized by scenes of humorous interactions between the landlady and the police. The main characters appear dithering and flighty, unlike the steely protagonists of later books. Millar must have realized this as a failed experiment because her remaining works banished the comical tone.

Her next book, *Vanish in an Instant*, showed Millar delving into topics that she would explore until the end of her career. Using autobiographical elements of place, the book is set in a Michigan college town during a terrible winter. The bleak atmosphere becomes a character in the book that evokes futility and darkness. The protagonist is trapped in a similar world, lost among people leading unful-filled lives.

Each character in *Vanish* has his or her own unfathomable problems. Earl Loftus, the man who confesses to a murder of a man he'd never met, is deformed with a cancer that leaves him with only months to live. Not only is the disease debilitating, he spends his last months constantly reminded of his mortality due to his bloated physical state. Loftus' landlady is irresistibly drawn to weak men and her husband has thousands of ambitious dreams, which will remain unfulfilled. Loftus' mother drinks heavily and loses time to blackouts and unconsciousness, but even she is tenderly portrayed by the lyric qualities of Millar's writing. "She wore short kid gloves, and protruding from the wrist of the right glove was her bus ticket. She had put it, not in her purse as a grown woman would, but in her glove for safe-keeping. It reminded Meecham of the Sunday School collection nickels he had carried when he was a boy, in the thumb of his mitten or the toe of his shoe; the uncomfortable, but wonderfully virtuous feeling…"[7] Despite the ease of drawing these characters as quirky misfits who are good for a chuckle, Millar brings them to life and makes the reader care for them. This depth to her writing made her something special in the field.

The plot itself is intricate. Virginia Hamilton Barkeley is accused of murdering her lover in a fit of passion. When Loftus confesses, the physical evidence corroborates his story. His unlikely admission holds enough details to make the police listen. However, Loftus has no motive and has never shown signs of a temper. Everyone tells his lawyer (first hired by Barkeley) that the crime was outside Loftus' nature. His only possible motive is a desire to do something grandiose before his death. Virginia, on the other hand, is a

---

7. Margaret Millar, *Vanish in an Instant* (New York: Random House, 1952). page 121.

strong-willed, spoiled debutante who sits in prison for two days rather than answer questions from the police. The characters' temperaments are complementary, but equally unattractive.

Vanish in an Instant paved the way for Millar's best work to that time. *Beast in View* won an Edgar for best novel in 1956. The central plot device shocked audiences with a little known psychological phenomenon, but over the years numerous other authors have recycled this device. Repetition has dulled its edge, meaning few have equaled Millar's original work. The plot is alarmingly simple. Evelyn Merrick has started a telephone campaign of terror against anyone who crosses her. Her specific wrath has been turned to the Clarvoe family which includes her childhood friend Helen who has become a hermit and Douglas, Evelyn's ex-husband, who admitted his homosexuality to his former wife only after their marriage. The phone harassment leads to suicide and murder and a startling discovery in the last few pages.

After the incredible success of *Beast in View*, the Millars moved from an apartment in Los Angeles to Santa Barbara, which would be their home until their deaths. Not only was Santa Barbara a writer's town at that point, it held the couple's interest by hosting a branch of the University of California, similar to the academic atmosphere of Ann Arbor where they had lived. Although Ken would later complete the doctorate he had begun at the University of Michigan, they tried to avoid the politics of the academic life on most counts. They taught occasional classes at UCSB and participated in the establishment of the Santa Barbara's Writers Conference. Mostly, they focused on local environmentalism.

Beast in View started a string of exceptional mystery novels for the author, modeled on the tragedies in her personal life. In February 1956, Millar's young daughter, Linda, was involved in an automobile accident. At just 16, she used the car given to her by her parents to run into three teenaged boys, killing one. The car also slammed into a parked car, throwing that driver sixty feet. The family immediately clammed up, hired an attorney, and pled the Fifth Amendment under oath at trial. By August of that year, the court ruled that Linda serve eight years of probation for her role in the accident. As part of the terms of her probation, she was ordered to undergo psychiatric treatment. The community of Santa Barbara was scandalized by the events, and Linda attempted suicide. Many residents of the town blamed the girl's condition on the dark, edgy writings of her parents.

At the same time, Ken Millar decided to try therapy. He'd been struggling with the traumas of his youth through his writings and wanted to get his demons under control once and for all. The simultaneous therapies put the Millars deeply in debt, but Margaret wanted to see her family at peace. Even one of their sources of income was threatened by the start of psychotherapy, as Ken wasn't sure that he would be able to write any more Lew Archer novels after settling his issues.

Ironically, *Beast* was the end of another series, tragic in its own way. Her Edgar for Best Novel was one of the final ones presented to a woman for nearly three decades. Ellis Peters and Celia Fremlin also won in the years before 1960, but a stark era commenced after that which would last until the early 1990s. Male writers and the hardboiled school of mysteries ruled the era from 1940 to 1975.

Millar was an independent, strong-minded woman, but even she could not have foreseen the ramifications of that particular streak. Sisters-in-Crime began in 1986 when several women mystery writers got together to complain about the lack of respect accorded to females in the profession. The thirty-some years since a woman's victory galvanized them into action as they realized the inequity of the situation in the MWA. Their efforts for equity have raised visibility for women authors. The result has been a major shift in the genre with more women writers present today and a renewed emphasis on readers that had been lacking prior to Sisters-in-Crime.

In *An Air That Kills*, the follow-up to *Beast in View*, Millar added social satire to her repartee. As usual, Millar wove details of interpersonal psychology into her work. Serial monogamy and infidelity rear their ugly heads with the story of a twice-married philandering husband who impregnates his best friend's wife. Most likely this came from Millar's experiences in Los Angeles and passing acquaintance with Southern California mystery authors like Stuart Palmer and Craig Rice who had more than a dozen unions between them. From the opening scenes of the book where the men friends have gathered for a weekend retreat, uneasiness pervades the writing. When Ron Galloway doesn't show for the weekend trip, the other guests chalk it up to poor manners or a guilty conscience over the affair.

As the days pass, Ron's disappearance becomes increasingly disturbing as the facts of the pregnancy and the explanation of Canadian divorce laws make for a scandalous and sticky situation. When Ron is found dead in his convertible along with a suicide note to his wife, the case comes to a close and the lives of the friends move on. In typical Millar fashion, only the last pages reveal the entire plot, which the reader has missed owing to the empathy for the characters. Strong arguments could be made that *An Air That Kills* is a mainstream novel with criminal overtones; such is the tone of the book. No formal detection takes place and no criminal charges stem from the denouement.

In this book, Millar returns to psychology to discuss her protagonists, but she doesn't use any new diagnoses to surprise the reader. By this time, she had learned a great deal about various theories of psychology coming from her role in her family's ongoing therapy. She lets two characters discuss it:

"In such a frame of mind she'd be unlikely, I think, to accept the kind of pay-off you suggest."

"Why?"

"It might seem to her a reward for something she loathes herself for."

"You read too much psychology."

Birmingham permitted himself a small tight smile. "Not at all. I practice it."[8]

Millar takes the familiar theme of the love triangle and adds her own special touches. The characters come to life with added shades to their personality. Ron's current wife is his former mistress who gained her husband through adultery. The insecurities of her position are evident when she cannot enjoy the world she has stolen for herself. The cuckolded former husband refuses to believe Ron's betrayal and then becomes obsessive about his ex-wife. The new mistress possesses a fierce pride, which makes her want to stand alone even after her lover's death. The precision with which Millar draws these characters leaves them etched into the reader's psyche long after the book is finished.

The next three novels offered a rarely found literary trick, a trademark of Millar's brand of suspense. The three books employ a device difficult in the mystery writer's art. Each book withholds a key element of its solution until the last lines of the book. This is made more difficult by the fact that the entire solution must be revealed to the reader in detail without giving away the final clue or detail that brings the solution to a surprise conclusion. Ellery Queen had accomplished this difficult trick in *The French Powder Mystery* back in the early 1930s when he named the murderer with the last words of the book. However, this device had fallen into disuse by the time Millar

8. Millar, Margaret. *An Air That Kills* (New York: Random House, 1957). page 208.

wrote her best works.

The first of these books, *The Listening Walls*, deals with an overheard conversation in a Mexican hotel that leads to a suicide and indications of a murder plot. When Amy Kellogg and Wilma Wyatt vacation south of the border, Wilma plunges over the balcony of their shared room clutching a silver box that she had purchased for Amy's husband. Upon her return to San Francisco, Amy skips town, giving her family only a mysterious letter stating she wants some time alone to deal with the tragedy.

The first book using the last sentence technique was not the best of Millar's efforts. In order to force the ending's double twist, too much information is withheld from the reader. Millar accomplishes the device by having a great deal of the action take place off-stage. By moving the major events from the core of the book, the remaining action leaves a rather passive book that deals with the emotions and action of the minor characters. One chapter is written entirely with the reader not knowing the identity of one of the two passengers in an automobile. Amy's husband is feeling murderous toward his fellow rider, even though the reader cannot recognize or identify that person. The emotional state of the characters is hard for the readers to clarify when their identities are a mystery. With a gifted writer, only so much can be revealed without giving away the character's identity.

> "[H]e knew the dog wouldn't stop chasing her as long as she kept running. If he had had a free choice, he would have whistled the dog to heel, put him in the car, and driven on, leaving her to wander in the woods by herself until she dropped of exhaustion, But he had no choice. She was his hope as well as his despair.
>
> She had reached the creek and was about to cross when he caught up with her."[9]

Nonetheless, the characters are well drawn and interesting. However, the action necessary to the plot is told through flashbacks and minor players. Margaret does not make this same mistake in her later books.

The second book of this trio, *A Stranger in My Grave*, introduces Steve Pinata, the first private investigator to appear in Millar's work. Just as the success of her early novels helped launch her husband's career, she had been influenced by the California P.I. tradition of Lew Archer and others. The inevitable comparisons between Archer and Pinata came from the reviewers and fans. Millar stopped using Pinata after a few novels, tired of people not recognizing the basic differences in their works.

The book's plot concerns a young woman who dreams she sees her own tombstone, complete with a date of death four years in the past. While awake, she actually finds the same grave with a man's name on it. She hires Pinata to learn the dream's connection to the dead man and solve the mystery of her dreams. The young woman determines that the date must have some significance to appear in her dreams. She attempts to link the date to some psychic death in her life although she has no idea what it might be. Like the best of Ross Macdonald's work, the solution lies in the past in tangled family relationships that are not made completely clear until the book's last two words.

Not only does Millar use psychology in her mystery, she adds her own interesting thoughts on the human condition. One concept is time and its use in our society. In order to learn the significance of the death date on her tombstone, Pinata must reconstruct what happened to his client on a particular day in the past. The idea of what differentiates one day from another in a person's life runs through the work. By tracing checks, calendars, employment records and newspapers,

9. Margaret Millar, *The Listening Walls* (New York: Random House, 1959), page 206.

Pinata manages to stimulate his client's memories to help learn the truth about that date. The book challenges the reader to realize the precious commodity of time and how easily it is wasted.

The third novel of this group, and Millar's finest in many critics' opinion, is *How Like an Angel.* Joe Quinn, a former Reno casino cop, comes in contact with a California religious cult called the True Believers. Quinn is down on his luck after losing his money and girlfriend due to bad luck at the gambling tables. He accepts the case only to earn enough money to return to Reno, but his curiosity is stirred by the case. Millar doesn't go for a quick sketch of religious zealots, but instead gives an in-depth portrait of how each person came to join the cult. Sister Blessing, an older woman in the cult, persuades him to investigate the disappearance and possible death of a man named Patrick O'Gorman that occurred five years ago. Quinn finds a possible connection to an embezzlement case that led the daughter of the local elite to an extended prison term. As with the trick of the final sentence twist, the comparison to Ellery Queen crops up because of his own work in the concept of an isolated religious cult with *And On the Eighth Day.* The book is explained only in the last lines of the work.

Like many of Millar's best works, *How Like an Angel* tied in to a personal mystery. Margaret based the character of Quinn on a real-life detective, Armand Girola. In May of 1959, her daughter, Linda, created her own mystery. Linda had been having trouble at college, having received a number of school citations for alcohol violations. She left school at the University of California at Davis and went to a casino just across the border in Nevada. She told friends that she would hitchhike back to school, then disappeared. Linda still suffered from enormous guilt for her part in the auto accident that had resulted in a young man's death. Her disappearance sparked a national search for the girl. Ken Millar hired his own detectives (including Girola), and went on television to plead for her return.

During her disappearance, her parents were given hope that she wasn't dead by tracing checks she had written while gone. She was located unharmed in Reno, Nevada ten days later, but, similarly to Agatha Christie's disappearance, she claimed to be unable to recall the missing time period or how she had made it to Nevada. Linda's disappearance violated her parole conditions, but again she was able to receive a sentence of only psychiatric evaluation. Ken's health was severely strained by the ordeal. He was hospitalized with cardiac distress, severe hypertension, and gout. He recovered, after a long bout in the hospital and a grueling series of medications.

For Margaret, the ordeal came out in her writing. The adage that writing close to personal fear makes for good fiction holds true in this case. *The Fiend* ostensibly deals with the disappearance of the protagonist's daughter. The book deals with a released sex offender who begins to keep tabs on two little girls that he notices at a playground. From the first page, the reader feels the internal tension. Paroled child molester Charlie Gowan tries to make a life for himself without little children. The struggle over his obsession is detailed in the book, the interior monologue of trying to keep his curiosity under control and within the bounds of his parole.

Millar's work in this novel is breathtaking. She characterizes a small number of people in the novel whose lives have been affected by Charlie. The two little girls' adulterous fathers shatter their families. The unhappy marriages and the unrequited loves all come through without easing the underlying tension of the impending strike of a predator. Unlike many "issues" novels, Millar does not preach to the readers, so the reader is not hit with the full impact of her observations until the end of novel. Millar makes a powerful message through her characters, not through author intrusion or forced dialogue.

The book almost falls outside the category of mystery since there are no murders and not really even a credible threat of a corpse since Gowan molested, but never killed. In a later version of the work, Millar writes, "My husband once suggested that I sub-title this book *After Psychiatry, What?* It's a good question. Some day there might be a good answer, and one of the most baffling problems facing judges and law enforcement officials might be solved."[10]

The subject of missing children could not have been an easy one for Millar in 1963, so shortly after her own child disappeared. While presumably the Millars knew the truth about Linda's disappearance, her absence was never satisfactorily explained to the public. The troubles of her daughter plus the failing health of Macdonald pained Millar. The selection of topic was hardly coincidental. Her usual crime novels contained the requisite murder. The only death in *The Fiend* is a young child's innocence. Even without a corpse, the book was nominated for Best Novel in 1963, but lost to *The Spy Who Came in From the Cold* by John Le Carre.

Margaret took off six years after writing *The Fiend*. Starting in the mid-1960's, Millar worked at a slower pace. Personally, Margaret began to suffer the effects of poor eyesight and incipient blindness. She would state in later interviews that the ordeal with her daughter destroyed her concentration.

As her output decreased, Macdonald's work began to get some recognition. His novels, *The Moving Target* and *The Drowning Pool*, were made into films starring Paul Newman, bringing readers to his work. His books became commercial hits with the tie-ins to the films. His next book became a best-seller, going through eight hardcover printings. In 1965, Ken Millar was named President of Mystery Writers of America, almost a full decade after his wife.

The couple settled down to a relatively quiet domestic life in Santa Barbara. They helped found a chapter of the National Audubon Society. During Millar's hiatus, *The Los Angeles Times* named her a

---

10. Margaret Millar, *The Fiend* (New York: Random House, 1963). Introduction.

Woman of the Year in 1965. The Millar's home became a haven for wildlife and birds, a life that Margaret detailed in *The Birds and the Beasts Were Here*, which came out in 1968. The book was originally supposed to be Ken and Margaret's collaboration, but it didn't work out that way. Margaret wrote the book by herself. Frequently, *The Birds and the Beasts* is called an autobiography of Millar, though the book focuses on the household and Millar's growing interest in bird watching more than any real telling of her life history. In 1969, an oil well off the coast of Santa Barbara exploded, unleashing millions of gallons of crude oil into the ocean. Already active environmentalists, the Millars started to take time to write about their activities. Macdonald's book *Sleeping Beauty* is thematically related to the oil spill.

After opening a vein to write *The Fiend*, Millar turned to more mundane topics with her next book, which didn't come out until 1970. *Beyond this Point Are Monsters*, set in the San Diego area, offers a moving portrait of Chicanos in the region. The title refers to medieval maps that had the titular statement on the edge of the known world. *Beyond This Point are Monsters* was nominated for an Edgar for Best Novel, but lost to The Laughing Policeman by Maj Sjowall and Per Wahloo.

The Millars suffered a series of losses in the early 1970s that kept Margaret from writing another novel for six years. Their beloved home sat on the path of frequent California fires and was destroyed by one raging blaze in 1970. The couple had to rebuild their house and relure their two-winged friends.

The couple suffered another blow when their daughter Linda died in 1970 of natural causes in her sleep. At 31, she'd been married for several years and had a child. She'd become a nurse and Ken Millar frequently compared her to his mother who had watched over others. Her tumultuous life had taken a toll on the couple, but her death hit them even harder. The Millars seemed to collapse in on themselves after her death, rarely going out or socializing with others.

The time did have some bright spots though. In 1973, Ken Millar (who had never won an Edgar) was awarded the MWA Grand Master Award and the Popular Culture Association Award of Excellence.

In 1976, Margaret Millar's next book, *Ask for Me Tomorrow*, follows a young Hispanic lawyer, Tom Aragon, to Mexico on the trail of wealthy Gilda Lockwood Decker's missing first husband and his illegitimate son by their former maid, an illegal Mexican immigrant. Again Millar comes back to psychology and the mind by making the young boy mentally handicapped. He can only think of the present without a thought to what happened last week or before. With a plot so driven by what had happened eight years in the past, the character makes the reader think about the wisdom of living in the past as Gilda Decker does.

Decker lives with her second husband, a stroke victim who can't communicate other than through a series of hand motions. Her life is made up now of nurses and aides; she lives only by recounting stories of her early life to a man who can barely recognize his wife. In contrast, Aragon, who is married to a resident pediatrician, looks forward to the future and a life with his wife, Laurie.

The trail of Decker's first husband is cold after almost a decade, but the secondary players in Lockwood's life begin to turn up dead. Aragon seems to react to the situation around him, a catalyst for the death of these people. After scenes in Baja and a Mexican prison, Aragon reached the end of his quest and a surprising trick of identity worthy of Millar's best work.

Aragon returned in the next two novels, only the third time in her career that she used series characters. *The Murder of Miranda* has more humor than most of her work, centering on the rich widow of the title and the head lifeguard at a California Beach Club. Typical of Millar, the title doesn't become clear until the final words of the book. In *Mermaid*, Aragon is hired to find a mentally handicapped young woman, and for its first half, the novel reads like some of Macdonald's plots. The ending isn't up to her usual standards, but is still an above average mystery novel.

In 1980, her husband was diagnosed with Alzheimer's and the couple began to stay close to home. Margaret often referred to them as a pair of bookends: two writers, one blind, the other slipping into a dark world of dementia. Ken Millar died on July 11, 1983.

Ironically, that would be the same year that Margaret was named MWA Grand Master so that she joined her husband in this honor. 1983 also saw the release of her novel *Banshee*. The title of the book comes from the strange banshee-like noises that several of the main characters hear as they are struggling with their emotions in the wake of an 8 year-old who is found badly decomposed in the local forest. Like so many other of her later works, the novel dealt with the psychological impact of a young girl's death on a community. Annamay Hyatt was well-loved in the area in which she lived, and as a result, most everyone feels some degree of guilt for her death. Like so many of Millar's work, the actual crime becomes a frame by which she investigates the mysteries of human behavior through crime and punishment.

She would publish one more novel, *Spider Webs*, which, on the surface, is a courtroom procedural. Cully Paul King is accused of murdering a wealthy socialite on the yacht that he captains. The woman accompanied him on an overnight stay aboard the yacht and she disappears the next day without a trace. Her body is discovered weeks later in a kelp bed, drowned and naked. Cully appears to be the only suspect in the case.

The entire book takes place during the course of the trial, featuring the point of view of many of the major characters in the book. The irony of the case is that each of the separate stories seems to have little to do with King's guilt or innocence. The characters have merely accommodated the trial in the midst of their own troubles.

The defense attorney is more concerned with his pill-addicted wife. The judge is afraid of quickly becoming irrelevant in his own court and contemplates outrageous legal decisions to take back the power in the situation. The court clerk is attracted to the defendant and not sure what to do about the situation. The unfolding personal dramas become more engrossing than the trial after the midpoint of the book. The reader wants to find the resolutions to the personal dilemmas of the characters as well as learn what really happened aboard the yacht. The book exposes the myth of the impartial justice system and shows that the system consists of fallible human beings.

Spider Webs was Millar's last book. She would live for 11 more years, relying on a medical assistant to aid her with the household duties as she became legally blind. She died at her Santa Barbara home on March 29, 1994.

Similar Authors Published Today:

- Jonathan Kellerman
- James Patterson
- Alex Matthews
- Stephen White
- Martha C. Lawrence
- Sarah Lovett
- Maxine O'Callaghan

Bibliography

The Invisible Worm - - - - - - - - - - - 1941
The Weak-Eyed Bat - - - - - - - - - - - 1942
The Devil Loves Me - - - - - - - - - - - 1942
Wall of Eyes - - - - - - - - - - - - - - 1943
Fire Will Freeze - - - - - - - - - - - - 1944
The Iron Gates - - - - - - - - - - - - - 1945
(aka Taste of Fears)
Experiment in Springtime - - - - - - - - 1947
It's All in the Family - - - - - - - - - - 1948
The Cannibal Heart - - - - - - - - - - - 1949
Do Evil in Return - - - - - - - - - - - 1950
Rose's Last Summer - - - - - - - - - - - 1952
Vanish in an Instant - - - - - - - - - - 1952
Wives and Lovers - - - - - - - - - - - 1954
A Beast in View - - - - - - - - - - - - 1955
(Edgar Winner)
An Air That Kills- - - - - - - - - - - - 1957
(aka The Soft Talkers)
The Listening Walls - - - - - - - - - - 1959
A Stranger in My Grave - - - - - - - - - 1960
How Like an Angel - - - - - - - - - - - 1962
The Fiend - - - - - - - - - - - - - - - 1964
Beyond This Point Are Monsters - - - - - 1970
Ask for Me Tomorrow - - - - - - - - - - 1976
The Murder of Miranda - - - - - - - - - 1979
Mermaid - - - - - - - - - - - - - - - - 1982
Banshee - - - - - - - - - - - - - - - - 1983
Spider Webs - - - - - - - - - - - - - - 1986

CHAPTER 2 — Leslie Ford

Leslie Ford was just one pen name of the prolific Zenith Jones Brown. The author of over 40 mystery novels under multiple pseudonyms wrote romantic, cozy mysteries with a strong sense of place and a keen eye for social justice. Throughout her series, Ford discussed the issues of her day within the confines of the plots she'd developed. Her books posed questions about the threat of Communism, freedom of the press, and rape—all while the hero falls madly for the woman in distress.

The importance of social justice in Ford's life started with her childhood. She was born in Smith River, Del Norte County, California in 1898, the youngest of 11 children in the family. Her given name was a corruption of the biblical Nitzenith, the mother of David. Ford was the daughter of the Reverend Milnor Jones, a missionary. Her family had relocated to California from Maryland to work with the local native Americans. The family moved often to further the Reverend Jones' mission with Western indigenous people.

Shortly after her birth, the family moved to Tacoma, Washington where Zenith attended high school and college, majoring in English. She received a B.A. from the University of Washington. She taught English at the University of Washington until she moved east.

She'd met her future husband during college. Ford K. Brown, a few years older than his bride-to-be, had been a friend of her brother's. Zenith Jones and Ford K. Brown renewed their friendship. Brown's education had been interrupted by World War I. After graduation, Ford K. Brown went to England to study for three years as a Rhodes Scholar. Meanwhile, Zenith moved to New York City where she took a job at *Dial Magazine* as circulation manager. After Ford K. Brown's return, the couple dated for two years, then married. The pair traveled Europe for a year, funded by an inheritance from Zenith's mother. The Browns returned to the United States because Ford K. had been offered a job at St. John's College in Annapolis, teaching English.

Maryland grew to hold a special place in Zenith's heart. Their daughter, Janet, was born there. Following Janet's birth, Professor Brown received a Guggenheim Fellowship, which required the family to go abroad again for his studies on the writer William Godwin.

While living in England, Ford decided to write her first book. *The Murder of An Old Man* was written under the pseudonym of David Frome and was published only in the U.K. in 1929. After writing two more mysteries as Frome, she was offered an American publishing contract. However, *The Murder of An Old Man* did not appear in an American edition because Brown thought it too simple for her growing audience. "[I]t had a secret passage, it had a woman with a wig, but it sold very well, but we just decided not to have it published here."[1]

She also used pen names to hide her gender. She would continue this tradition throughout her career. The Frome name came from her husband's father. "the David Frome name – Frume is the way it should be pronounced – I chose it because it was a compliment to my husband's father, his name was David and Frome was a little village down in Somerset where we were staying at the time... So that's how

---

1. Oral History interview, Zenith Jones Brown, 1976, page 18, Oral History Collection, Maryland Historical Society. Hereafter cited as Brown, M.H.S.

I chose that."[2]

Mystery stories seemed like a natural choice for Zenith. Her father had read all of the Sherlock Holmes stories to her as a girl and her husband was a fan of more modern detective stories. Additionally, one of Ford's English friends inspired her when the friend published a mystery novel of her own. Brown decided that she could write a novel as well.

The prolific writer started without any plan of making a career of writing. "[T]he reason that I wrote that book was that everything cost so much more in England to live than you had any idea of."[3] Within a year, she had produced three novels with British settings.

Ford started her career in a humorous way. She told the story of a family friend who knew the first publisher to whom she had sent the manuscript. After going for a visit to the publisher and not discovering the book in the slush piles, the friend found the pages by the trashcan. The family friend rescued the pages and took them to an acquaintance at Methuen Publishing, where the book was snapped up.

Ford's quick writing style meant that she would have at least one book published every year for almost two decades. Ford wrote her first mystery in six weeks. The sale of the first prompted her to write two more books under the Frome name. "The thing that is hardest about writing, for me anyway, was giving up all of the other things that I was doing—closing the door and not answering the phone and sitting at it 8 hours a day—getting down to it at nine o'clock in the morning and getting up at five, and not waiting for inspiration to strike. I learned that that was a mistake. If you waited for inspiration, you'd never write at all."[4]

Her first efforts under the Frome name dealt with Scotland Yard and the British police. Most, but not all of her later Frome books, feature Mr. Evan Pinkerton, a feisty Welshman, who teams up with Scotland Yard to solve crimes. "Mr. Pinkerton, I certainly never ex-

---

2. Brown, M.H.S., page 28
3. Brown, M.H.S., page 18.
4. Brown, M.H.S., page 25.

pected him to become as important in a story as he was. But, after a while, I began to write a story largely from his point-of-view, so he became the main character in the story, but I know who did it and why, and I don't always know how, but usually I do."[5]

The Evan Pinkerton series is pretty standard Golden Age detective fare. From the poorer classes, Pinkerton yearns for adventure and intrigue. His short stature adds to his notion that people look down on him and his ethnicity as a Welshman in British culture makes him stand out more. Pinkerton is teamed with Inspector Bull from Scotland Yard, a more intimidating presence. The name "Bull" is reflective of the British paternal archetype of John Bull, a visible symbol of England's international power as well as slang for policeman. Yet, Pinkerton has his own tenacious methods that usually lead him to the solution of the mystery.

In several of the mysteries, Ford (as Frome) uses the class difference as both humor and social commentary. Pinkerton relies more on intuition and perseverance than stunning brainpower, and he is the frequent subject of social humiliation. While the books use the same conventions as many of the English cozies, as an American Ford wrote about the British class system with a slightly different perspective. The Frome titles didn't treat working class people in a patronizing manner. More empathy was provided for the blue-collar men who made social gaffes in the company of lords and ladies.

The prolific author adopted a second pen name when she wrote about the United States. This new series took place in her beloved Maryland, near Washington, D.C. Not only were the books popular, the magazine market began serializing them. *The Lady's Home Journal* published three of her early novels, adding to her popularity in the U.S. Ford soon employed the fast pace and cliffhangers chapter endings of serialization in writing subsequent books.

The first novels written under the Leslie Ford nom de plume were standalone romantic mysteries with certain features in common. While the plots were decidedly mystery, the primary motivation of the

---

5. Brown, M.H.S, page 63.

characters was romance with an eye towards matrimony. The characters fall in love quickly and deeply, with some unusual pairings. Additionally, the books are all set in the Chesapeake Bay area with special attention to the flora and fauna of the region. In *The Clue of the Judas Tree*, Louise Cather goes to Ivy Hill, the Trent family estate in Maryland to record the life of Duncan Trent for a biography. Her job is cut short when Trent is murdered. Blame falls on Michael Spur, the young man who had murdered his father in a delusional state at Ivy Hill many years ago. He'd been cured of his mental problems and returned to see Cheryl Trent, the daughter of the victim.

The standalone books are interesting in that the reader does not expect some of the romantic pairings made. Cheryl falls for the man who has supposedly killed her father. While the romance adds a reason to solve the crimes quickly, Cheryl's infatuation seems ill-timed at best. By the end of the book, the narrator, Louise, has expressed interest in a man who she had previously judged a gigolo and a possible murderer. The reader is asked to forgive these suspicions and view them as a happy couple.

Ford continued writing the romantic cozy mysteries at a fast pace, producing two or three books a year. In *The Town Cried Murder*, the setting is historic Williamsburg, Virginia. While the narrative takes place in current day, the shadows of three hundred years of history lay over the story. The heroine, Faith Yardley, seems to live under a curse. Her two fiancées are brutally murdered in the course of days. Faith's first intended is killed, and she accepts the proposal of another man in less than 24 hours. The characters have a remarkable resilience in matters of love. While admittedly, Faith doesn't fancy her first two suitors in a romantic way, she makes commitments to them to save the family home (a la *Gone with the Wind* and Mr. Kennedy). The thwarted characters watch Faith steal the object of their affection, giving them the motives for the murders. By the end of the book, Yardley is engaged for a third time to her true love, Bill Haines.

The book has a fascinating background in the restored town and Ford makes good use of its historical setting. She incorporates details of how the Restoration Society purchased homes and makes the

Yardleys' refusal to sell a motive for murder. Characters dress up in Colonial garb for the tourists and the transient nature of the tourists allow for hidden backgrounds and secrets.

Within a few books, Ford moved to a series character for her romantic pairing. Most of the Leslie Ford novels feature Colonel Primrose, a retired military man, and Grace Latham, a small town woman with a knack for stumbling into murder. Primrose is accompanied by his stoic sidekick, Sergeant Phineas T. Buck, another military man who eyes Latham's role in the Colonel's life with suspicion. In the early books, Primrose and Buck remind the reader of other police duos, like Van Dine's District Attorney Markham and Sergeant Heath or Ellery Queen's Inspector Queen and Sergeant Velie. Latham serves as the first-person narrator in the books with Primrose and Buck as the real sleuths. In some cases, Latham actually tries to thwart the solution by hiding evidence or not sharing all she knows. She believes that in doing so, she is helping the cause of true love. Although sometimes amused by her antics, Primrose is never deceived and solves the crimes without Latham's full cooperation. The pair complement each other well, making for a pleasant read.

The earliest adventures of Colonel Primrose don't feature the relationship between the two characters. One of his first appearances is in *The Clock Strikes Twelve*, which features the familiar Washington D.C. environs where most of Ford's books were set. The killer murders his victim in the Supreme Court chambers. Ford would write eight such novellas for *The American Magazine* in the 1930s. *The Strangled Witness* appeared in 1934 with only Colonel Primrose.

In the first book of the Primrose / Latham series, *Ill Met by Moonlight*, the action occurs at April Harbor, a small town on the eastern shore of Chesapeake Bay. Ford uses her knowledge of the area to bring a comforting realism to the book's environment. Her descriptions of place are evocative, yet tightly written. Mrs. Latham owns a cottage in April Harbor, near the home of the first victim. Colonel Primrose and his constant companion, Sergeant Buck, lodge with Mrs. Latham because of a shortage of rooms in town. Future books would have Latham and Primrose living on the same street in Georgetown.

At the center of *Ill Met by Moonlight* are two couples with star-crossed lovers as half of each couple. The title is appropriate as it is a quote from *A Midsummer Night's Dream*, which features four lovers in a lovers' quadrangle. The book uses a similar romantic entanglement between the major characters to force them to resolve the situation by the end of the book. However, in a Ford novel, the odd person out in the relationship is usually dead by the end of the book.

The typical Ford book features a couple presented with a huge obstacle to true love. Usually the obstacle is a person blocking the relationship in some manner. That person doesn't survive beyond the first few chapters. In *Ill Met by Moonlight*, the obstacle to happiness is Sandra Gould, the wife of Jim Gould. When Jim is reunited with his childhood sweetheart, Rosemary Bishop, Sandra's fate is sealed. Ford tries to make Sandra unpalatable, so that the reader is not disturbed when she is bludgeoned to death in the garage. Sandra, who is described as a "Eurasian Mae West," refuses to divorce Jim despite her many infidelities. Sandra presents a problem to the couple first by her existence. Later her murder casts suspicion on both Jim and his intended, Rosemary. Of course, the couple begins to doubt the innocence of their respective lovers. They do foolish things to cover up including half-hearted confessions. The crime must be properly solved so that the young couple can find their way back to each other. While some might consider it callous to emotionally recover in the course of a few days, Jim and Rosemary rekindle their romance and decide to marry by the end of the book.

Most Ford books have at least one couple, and sometimes two that decide to live happily ever after by the end of the book. Despite the travails that meet these romantic leads during the events of the book, the characters can easily be eliminated as suspects and potential murder victims. Happy couples may be arrested, but they are never guilty of murder. This presents a problem for Ford as a writer, since so many of the characters are already spoken for. Her modus operandi often lies with the least likely suspect in the case, since the main players cannot be guilty.

Besides the romantic interests, a heavy amount of foreshadowing also takes place in the books, but not enough to be classified in the heroine-in-distress (or "Had I But Known") school of writing. The books open with the familiar foreboding that perhaps if Mrs. Latham had known what would happen, she might have done things different-ly. "It was fantastic from the beginning, or would have been anywhere except in Washington, or at any time here before now, when things we've always thought fantastic seem to have become normal and have a kind of horrible validity. And I'm not thinking about the end of it so much as the beginning that made Sylvia Peele point out in her script that the party could only have happened in Washington."[6] Even though Grace Latham sometimes acts impetuously to protect romance, she is a cautious woman by nature and doesn't take unnecessary risks. She's not one to investigate a dark alley at night by herself.

In *Ill Met by Moonlight*, Ford manages to juggle four separate tumultuous relationships in the course of the book. Jim and Rosemary, Andy and Lucy Lee, Mrs. Gould and Mr. Bishop, and the introduction of the ongoing romance between Mrs. Latham and Colonel Primrose.

The romance between Mrs. Latham and Colonel Primrose is certainly one of the slowest moving in mystery fiction. After their ini-tial meeting in *Ill Met by Moonlight*, the couple does virtually nothing about their relationship over the course of many more books. They be-come constant companions, but often argue with each other over solv-ing crimes. Mrs. Latham puts the people she cares about above the law and is not above lying, sneaking out, or hiding evidence to assist a young couple in jeopardy. Colonel Primrose is another matter. He is often described as a man who would gladly hang his own grandmother if he found her guilty of a crime. There's little room in his world for moral ambiguity. Even though Colonel Primrose is seldom fooled by Mrs. Latham's actions, he rarely condemns her deeds and pre-empts her on more than one occasion with the willing help of Sergeant Buck.

There are other obstacles to their personal relationship. The most obvious impediments to the couple are Sergeant Buck and the

---

6. Leslie Ford, *The Murder of a Fifth Columnist* (New York: Charles Scribner's Sons, 1940), page 7.

Latham boys. Sergeant Buck has an overactive sense of loyalty to the Colonel and makes no bones about his distrust of all women. In *Ill Met by Moonlight*, he actually cautions Mrs. Latham not to accept any proposals from the Colonel. Even when Buck has a flirtation in *Old Lover's Ghost*, he never lets up on his disapproval of Mrs. Latham. The Latham children are no better about meting out approval of the relationship, mostly because of the pair's age difference.

Despite the disapproval, Washington society accepts them as a couple, and they frequently are invited to the same parties and social functions. Despite the flirtations and the obvious forbearance of the Colonel in putting up with Mrs. Latham's skirting of the law, the relationship moves glacially. After four years and eight books, the Colonel does muster a half-hearted proposal, which Mrs. Latham quickly brushes off.

The Latham / Primrose series came years before the glut of mystery heroines who date a policeman, but this series in the 1940s and 1950s helped pave the way for so many others in the second Golden Age. Ford's books were among the earliest examples of the romantic pairings that would come to be a hallmark of the early days of the mystery's re-emergence. While the situation is not used as frequently today, many of the series that started in the 1980s are still being written today.

It's easy to see why the "women who date policemen" structure was used so frequently. This relationship model allows the heroine access to a number of crime scenes and all the evidence that a normal civilian would not be privy to. While Primrose doesn't reveal all that he knows to Latham, she acts as both a Watson and Irene Adler to his Holmes. Modern crime scene investigation would not allow for civilians to go bumbling across a crime scene. Yet accompanied by a member of the police, the heroine gets an inside view of the investigation, usually synopsized by her boyfriend.

The situation allows for character growth and relationship growth at the same time, giving the characters depth as the reader sees into how the characters function with their significant others. The pairing puts the two characters at odds, since the police are going by strict rules on what can be done. The heroine has no such proscriptions on her behavior, so she can come and go as she pleases. The resulting friction gives more insight into how the characters handle conflict and resolution.

The scenario has been used frequently to make the situation of an amateur sleuth more believable to the readers who might worry about the number of corpses discovered by a housewife and mother. There's no indication in the early books of the series that Latham had ever run across a corpse prior to her introduction to Colonel Primrose. While she gains a certain aplomb in running across dead bodies, Latham's first instinct is to call the police in the form of Colonel Primrose.

The early Latham / Primrose novels started with domestic scenarios. The next book in the series, *False to Any Man,* deals with a young ward who is provided everything at the expense of the guardian's biological children, the Candlers. The guardian's daughter is half of a young couple torn apart by the ward. When the ward is found murdered, the pair are certain that the other has killed the girl. Mrs. Latham meddles in the investigation by living with the Candlers until the crimes are solved.

Ford delineates social class in this book, much as she did in the Evan Pinkerton series. In the novel, she shows the well-heeled ward of dubious origins in direct comparison to the genteel poverty of the Candlers, who have reputation if little else. Judge Candler feels sorry for his ward, because the upbringing cannot compensate her for a good name, like their own family's name.

Additionally, the book begins the more political overtones that would creep into the series with the onset of World War II. Judge Candler is being considered for a position on the Supreme Court, and the taint of scandal could ruin his chances for appointment. So the crimes have to be quickly and discreetly solved before the press can take aim at him.

Still operating in a domestic environment albeit a more natural one, Grace Latham and her son go west in *Old Lover's Ghost.* While Latham's two sons are frequently mentioned, they rarely appear "in person" in the books. The series watches them mature from school-boys to college men to soldiers fighting in the war. *Old Lover's Ghost* takes place in Yellowstone Park and features a number of park rangers in the book. The book has a tinge of early environmentalism with the lectures from the rangers on the damage to Yellowstone from the tourists and pollution concerns. The mystery is overshadowed by all the other doings, including Sergeant Buck's dalliance with a gold-digging woman.

The books take a decidedly more political turn starting with *The Murder of a Fifth Columnist* and the first rumblings of World War II. With the turn towards government and politics, the books become more serious in tone and subject matter. The impending involvement of the United States in World War II was a primary topic in Washington at that time and so it appeared in the books as well. "People used to say Piccadilly Circus was the hub of the universe, and if you stood on the corner by the Cafe Royal long enough everybody in the world would pass by. Now that Piccadilly Circus is rimmed with bombed-out, boarded-up windows, Washington has pretty much taken over, and it seems one doesn't have to wait long to see the world, in the French sense at least, not pass by, but come apparently to stay."[7]

The Murder of a Fifth Columnist deals with the leaking of government and U.S. military secrets in regard to the United States' preparedness just before World War II. An anonymous newsletter is being spread around Washington that contains information on the military build-up and it is damaging morale. People in the armed services want to plug the leak before too much is shared with Axis intelligence, but many of the characters are newspaper reporters who talk at length about free speech and the rights of the press in a democracy. The book doesn't provide any easy answers, but the reader is given a lot to think about, topics still relevant almost 60 years after it was written.

The next book in the series, *Murder in the O.P.M.*, takes place in the Office of Production Management. The distribution of prometh-

---

7. Leslie Ford, *All For the Love of a Lady* (New York: Charles Scribner's Sons, 1943) page 63.

ium, a mythical minor metal, has taken on new importance in the production of war materials. In one of the rare instances that Primrose actually involves Mrs. Latham in a crime, he requests that she host a dinner for the head of the O.P.M. at her house. "For all the people who think it improbable, not to say improper, for a woman to be involved with – at the least – more than one murder and still be invited out to dinner, I would like to say that this time it was entirely Colonel Primrose's fault."[8]

The department head is murdered before the dinner can occur, but Mrs. Latham gets involved anyway. The book deals with the subject of war profiteering and the types of corporate businessmen who decide to make a profit for themselves at the cost of the war effort. The business people do not fare well in the book, as they are the source of the trouble as well as the murder victims.

Despite her prodigious output writing for the Latham / Primrose series, Ford still took time to write standalone books as well. With *Murder With Southern Hospitality*, Ford moves beyond her typical Maryland environs to go south to Natchez, Mississippi. The book takes place at a home and garden show where the main characters have gone for a visit. Miss Letty, one of the pilgrims, is originally from Mississippi. The other two women are amazed to find that Letty, who now lives cheaply, hails from the largest, prettiest plantation in town. The book suffers in transferring its location, which seems stilted and stereotyped at times. The Southern characters are drawn broadly to type with less attention to detail than in her Maryland books.

The crimes begin with the murder of one of the visitors who has become too nosy into the affairs of Miss Letty and her family, the Draytons. The family has been put in an awkward position by the will of Uncle Minot who insists that Anne Drayton, the young heir to the plantation, marry Steve Heywood, a fighter pilot and former resident of Natchez. Though the pair don't meet for several chapters, they are instantly intrigued by each other while the family struggles to keep them apart.

---

8. *Leslie Ford, Murder In The O.P.M.* (New York: Charles Scribner's Sons, 1942), page 5.

Ford returned to Latham and Primrose in *All for the Love of a Lady*, which deals with the black market and people who profiteer from the war effort abroad. Cass Crane, who married just before he left for war, comes home to investigate a vague plot concerning government goods being purchased on the cheap by foreign businessmen. The plot is tied up with his ex-girlfriend, Courtney, who is now married to shady businessman D.J. Durbin. This arrangement doesn't please Molly Crane, Cass' wife, who is jealous of his focus on another woman. When Durbin is murdered, Cass is implicated and has to prove his innocence. While Molly doesn't believe that her husband is a killer, she stays with Grace instead of going home. Through the course of the series, Grace Latham hosts any number of unhappily married women who don't want to return to their husbands.

The book takes on a more moralist tone as the Cranes are reunited at the end of the book. Courtney Durbin is left with money, but no love. It's obvious from the tone of the writing, which person Ford thinks will be happiest.

In another standalone, *Date With Death*, Dr. Jonas Smith finds the body of a Hollywood publicist, Gordon Grymes, who had lured a high school girl to a remote cabin for a tryst. The young girl is the sister of Smith's romantic interest, giving him a reason to keep the situation hidden from the police. Grymes had a nasty habit of taking his date to a secluded place and then throwing away the car keys. His routine is to hand the girl a gun and tell her to use it on him or submit to his advances. The high school girl fires the gun and runs off in a panic.

The book progresses with typical Ford attention to Annapolis and the region. The girl's brother is a midshipman who is implicated in the crime and punished for sneaking off the military base. The murder takes place at some vacation cottages by the shore and the book goes into detail on the local flora. In fact, Ford uses that information as a clue to the solution of the murder.

Ford revisited the social issue of rape in *Trial by Ambush*. She would later recall, "in *Trial by Ambush*, it was about the rape and the rapist is real crazy and he's in police headquarters because he wants to see the girl come in when she goes into the lineup. The sergeant grabs him and puts him in the lineup by accident. You have to read it twice, you know, because it's like the rapist was confused by being asked to go inside and so, he's mixed up. He doesn't want to do that. So, the reader is confused for a minute."[9]

Ford's efforts to write about social issues did not stop there. In 1947, she wrote *The Woman in Black*. The book takes a look at growth of industrial capitalism that stemmed from the war years, the structure that Eisenhower would later call "the military-industrial complex". The first chapters of the novel debunk the notion that "what's good for GM is good for America." Ford portrays the robber baron as little more than a egotistical con man, driven by pride and greed. "This man acts as if he thought he was a cross between Henry Ford, Henry Kaiser, Henry Garsson, and Henry VIII."[10] Stubblefield is contemplating a bid for the presidency of the United States, making for a scarier scenario with this man running the country for his own material purposes.

In this book, the search for synthetic rubber is discussed in terms of what impact such an invention would have on the economy and industry in America. Of course, the manufacture of chemical substitutes for rubber would have made the war go in a different way, perhaps without rationing. Would a nation that is not deprived of staples have pushed as hard to win the war? Would the U.S. have dropped the bomb?

The unscrupulous Stubblefield goes to great lengths to try to obtain the process. For all the discussion of the chemical process, Ford doesn't even try to get into the details of chemical engineering, having Mrs. Latham disclaim at one point, "I don't even know what a polymer is."

In contrast, the book positively portrays the value of real interpersonal relationships. The friendship between protagonist Grace Latham and the young woman who looks for her help is accepted as fact, so that the friend, Susan Kent, is cleared in Grace's mind of all indiscretions. Grace excludes her from suspicion. Not only does this

9. Brown, M.H.S., page 66.

10. Leslie Ford, *The Woman in Black* (New York: Charles Scribner's Sons, 1947), page 53.

provide Grace with an ally, Ford shows the power of interpersonal relationships against a backdrop of rampant capitalism.

While Ford would never have referred to it as such, there's a strong sense of feminism in the Latham / Primrose series as well. The women in the books are well-written and strongly portrayed. As part of a social network in Washington, the women in the books provide the grease that runs the society. The men might have the positions of power and the titles, but behind most every man in Ford's books is a woman who knows what is going on and tries to protect society as a whole. Ironically so, the women of the books are portrayed as the more lawless part of the population as they hide clues and physical evidence to protect those they love.

For all her discussions of social issues, Ford never touched on civil rights in her books. Despite writing under a man's name, Ford never found that air of gender discrimination in her career. "[I]t's always been from men that I have gotten all the encouragement and all the help that I ever needed... men publishers, men editors, my husband, a critic. I have always thought that they were more than anxious to help a woman who was trying to do something. That's been my experience with them. I think they are wonderful."[11]

Even with her progressive ideas and the social ideals brought forth in her works, Ford didn't manage much in the way of progressive thought with the treatment of blacks in her work. She uses the stereotypical language and traits of the servant class in her works. Though she portrays Mrs. Latham's cook, Lilac, as a woman of great loyalty, the servant is still painted with the same brush as many of the other servants characterized in the novels. Her character speaks in a rather demeaning dialect and Lilac is portrayed as having blind faith in religion. All of the blacks seem to have the same dialect and speech patterns. Like the women in the novels, this underclass has its own network that proves faster and more accurate than the police.

Trial by Ambush, in 1962, was Ford's last book written under the pen name of Leslie Ford. Her other series under the Frome name

11. Brown, M.H.S., page 19.

had stopped a decade prior. After their many years of travel, Ford and her husband settled permanently in Annapolis, Maryland. They also owned a farm on the eastern shore, where Ford relaxed with horses when not writing.

Ford lived another two decades in relative retirement. She died on August 25, 1983. Her papers were donated to St. John's College in Maryland and mystery author Marcia Talley acts as her unofficial literary executor.

Similar Authors Published Today:

- Lora Robert
- Janet Evanovich
- Jill Churchill
- Diane Mott Davidson
- Jonnie Jacobs
- Evan Marshall
- Nancy Pickard
- Joan Hess
- Jeanne M. Dams
- Carola Dunn
- Sara Hoskinson Frommer
- Tamar Myers
- Marcia Talley

Bibliography

As Leslie Ford

  The Sound of Footsteps - - - - - - - - - 1931
  (UK Title: Footsteps on the Stairs)
  Murder in Maryland - - - - - - - - - - - 1932
  By the Watchman's Clock - - - - - - - - - 1932
  The Clue of the Judas Tree - - - - - - - - 1933
  The Strangled Witness - - - - - - - - - - 1934
  Burn Forever - - - - - - - - - - - - - - 1935
  (UK Title: Mountain Madness)
  Ill Met by Moonlight - - - - - - - - - - - 1937
  The Simple Way of Poison - - - - - - - - 1937
  Three Bright Pebbles - - - - - - - - - - 1938
  Reno Rendezvous - - - - - - - - - - - - 1939
  (UK Title: Mr. Cromwell Is Dead)
  False to Any Man - - - - - - - - - - - - 1939
  (UK Title: Snow-White Murder)
  The Town Cried Murder - - - - - - - - - 1939
  Old Lover's Ghost - - - - - - - - - - - - 1940
  (UK Title: A Capital Crime)
  Road to Folly, 1940
  The Murder of a Fifth Columnist, 1941
  Murder in the O.P.M. - - - - - - - - - - 1942
  (UK Title: Priority Murder)
  Murder with Southern Hospitality - - - - - 1942
  (UK Title: Murder Down South)
  Siren in the Night- - - - - - - - - - - - - 1943
  All for the Love of a Lady - - - - - - - - 1944
  (UK Title: Crack of Dawn)
  The Philadelphia Murder Story - - - - - - 1945
  Honolulu Story - - - - - - - - - - - - - 1946
  (UK Title: Honolulu Murder Story. Also: Honolulu Murders)
  The Woman in Black - - - - - - - - - - - 1947
  The Devil's Stronghold - - - - - - - - - - 1948
  Date with Death - - - - - - - - - - - - - 1949
  (UK Title: Shot in the Dark)
  Murder Is the Pay-Off - - - - - - - - - - 1951
  The Bahamas Murder Case - - - - - - - 1952

Washington Whispers Murder - - - - - - 1953
(UK Title: The Lying Jade)
Invitation to Murder - - - - - - - - - - - - 1954
Murder Comes to Eden - - - - - - - - - - 1955
The Girl from the Mimosa Club - - - - - - 1957
Trial by Ambush - - - - - - - - - - - - - 1962
(UK Title: Trial from Ambush)

As Brenda Conrad

The Stars Give Warning - - - - - - - - - - 1941
Caribbean Conspiracy - - - - - - - - - - 1942
Girl with a Golden Bar - - - - - - - - - - 1944

As David Frome

The Murder of an Old Man - - - - - - - - 1929
In at the Death - - - - - - - - - - - - - - 1929
The Hammersmith Murders - - - - - - - - 1930
Two Against Scotland Yard - - - - - - - - 1931
(UK Title: The By-Pass Murder)
The Strange Death of Martin Green - - - - 1931
(UK Title: The Murder on the Sixth Hole)
The Man from Scotland Yard - - - - - - - 1932
(UK Title: Mr. Simpson Finds a Body)
The Eel Pie Murders - - - - - - - - - - - 1933
(UK Title: Eel Pie Mystery)
Scotland Yard Can Wait! - - - - - - - - - 1933
(UK Title: That's Your Man, Inspector!)
Mr. Pinkerton Goes to Scotland Yard - - - 1934
(UK Title: Arsenic in Richmond)
Mr. Pinkerton Finds a Body - - - - - - - - 1934
(UK Title: The Body in the Turf)
Mr. Pinkerton Grows a Beard - - - - - - - 1935
(UK Title: The Body in Bedford Square)
Mr. Pinkerton Has the Clue - - - - - - - - 1936
The Black Envelope - - - - - - - - - - - - 1937
(UK Title: The Guilt Is Plain)
Passage For One - - - - - - - - - - - - - 1938
Mr. Pinkerton at the Old Angel 1939
(UK Title: Mr. Pinkerton and the Old Angel)
Homicide House - - - - - - - - - - - - - - 1950
(UK Title: Murder on the Square)

CHAPTER 3 -- Phoebe A. Taylor

At a time when many mystery authors had turned to the hard-boiled genre, Phoebe Atwood Taylor followed her own comedic path. Under three different names, she wrote humorous regional mysteries set in New England. Although she began her career during the first Golden Age when humor was more prevalent, her wacky tales of intrigue allowed her to continue writing long after many cozy writers had fallen away. She gave up her career in 1951 after 33 books, but her works remain in print today.

Taylor was born on May 18, 1909 in Boston, surprisingly far from the peninsula she would call home for most of her life. Taylor later recalled that she was the first member of her family to be born off Cape Cod in over 300 years. Like many established New England clans, family mattered to the Taylors. She was an avid genealogist and knew her family's history back to the settlement of the Cape.

Taylor was a product of her practical forebears. Common sense Yankee ways were bred into her as she grew up. The region's no-nonsense, hard working ethics were second nature to someone from an established Cape family. At an early age, she showed signs of her future calling. In one of her earliest surviving letters, she wrote to her sea captain grandfather, Captain Joshua Nickerson Taylor. The sailor had traveled and traded around the world in the 1800s. His adventures intrigued the little girl with the big imagination.

Taylor left the Cape to attend college. She quickly made a name for herself in school. She was a Lucille Pulitzer scholar at Barnard College in New York, graduating in 1930. Her friends at Barnard described the young author as "a bland, imperturbable young woman with a Boston accent, an inquisitive pug nose, and a mind like a two-edged sword."[1]

Careers were scarce for strong-minded women during the Great Depression and Taylor found that writing suited her well. She moved back to Weston, Massachusetts, after graduation and began to write while caring for her invalid aunt, Alice Tilton. She split her time between writing and nursing her aunt. The enforced time at home allowed her plenty of hours to devote to her fiction. Her first mystery, *The Cape Cod Mystery*, appeared the following year when Taylor was 22 years old, an impressive feat for a young lady of any era.

Taylor was unique in many ways. She was eccentric. She routinely referred to herself in third person when writing, and often called herself PAT (her initials) in correspondence. She had a habit of doodling in the margins of her manuscripts and often left notes for herself at the edge of the pages. She chastised herself for not starting a book soon enough before deadline. She carped about her schedule and made plot notes.

Taylor indulged her love of Cape Cod by filling her home with reminders of her heritage. Taylor wrote in an office that had been decorated like her mother's own office/study, filled with antique dolls and children's books. Taylor was something of a packrat. She collected many things, including books by local authors and travel-related works. She later donated a significant portion of her personal library to Boston University along with her archival papers.

It was no surprise to anyone who knew her that Taylor's mys-

1. Katherine Kominis "Never Out of Style: Phoebe Atwood Taylor", *Firsts Magazine*, (November 1991): page 22.

tery took place on Cape Cod, a place she knew intimately and loved. Taylor prided herself on her knowledge of the Cape and its environs, details that she included in her novels. In *Spring Harrowing*, Taylor pokes fun at her own obsession by including a reference to an old Cape history book entitled *Quanomet My Quanomet* that is partially written in verse. The fictional tome becomes a vital clue as it relates the history of shipwrecks off the coast of Cape Cod. That same rich sense of place permeates Taylor's work.

Even her sleuth was a quintessential Cape Codder. *The Cape Cod Mystery* introduced Asey Mayo, a common-sense sleuth who would appear in 21 novels and two short story collections. Her first novel takes place in Wellfleet, Massachusetts, on the Cape. While a small peninsula town with a limited number of egresses does not seem like an ideal place for murder, Taylor fashioned her crimes to the location without problem. The isolated nature of the Cape makes the crimes a closed community that worked similar to the snowed-in weekend house murders of an earlier era.

The first book in the series featured many traits that Taylor would hone over the course of the series. The strongest component of her Asey Mayo books is its regional flavor. Taylor infused her love of the area into every paragraph. Visitors to the Cape still pick up copies of her books to get an idea of what to expect from the region.

Cape Cod was never an afterthought to the plot or characters. The characters speak with the dialect of the region, just enough to evoke the flavor of conversation without making the meaning impossible to decipher. Words like "keening", "wa-el", and "supposing I did" found their way into the dialog of her books. At one point, Mayo says, "Syl, it now behooves you an' me to find Mrs. Remington, without any maybein' about it. I'm beginning not to like this, an' I'm beginning to be a little mite worried. Let's go."[2] Without disrupting the action, Taylor seamlessly works in a healthy dollop of the unique flavor of the Northeastern pronunciations.

2. Phoebe Atwood Taylor, *Spring Harrowing* (New York: WW Norton & Co, 1939), page 66.

In contrast to the strong regionalism, the narrator of the first book was an outsider. *The Cape Cod Mystery* has a first person point-of-view character in Prudence Whitsby, a tourist for the season on the Cape. In the same manner that an outsider makes a great writer, a tourist can describe the Cape with admiring detail that a longtime resident could not. The sun, sand, and unique flora of the place are evoked more clearly from an outside perspective.

Through Prudence Whitsby's eyes, we first meet Asey Mayo, described as a friend of the Porters, the local first family. The Porters are a mainstay of Wellfleet and own the local automobile manufacturing plant. Porter automobiles will become a trademark of the Mayo series and the later Witherall series as well. Mayo is such a good friend to the Porter family that he's given free rein with the investigation and an unlimited budget to do so. Mayo sets an outrageous schedule of solving the murder of Dale Sanborn before Monday morning so that Bill Porter is not detained longer than necessary. Most of her later books would feature a similar time constraint, adding suspense with the knowledge that time was running out quickly for the accused.

This first book introduces Asey Mayo as the New England equivalent of a bon vivant. Mayo has been a handyman, sailor, cook, racecar driver, and Porter automobile designer. He is frequently darting around the roads of Wellfleet in his Porter roadster. Though he has family in the area, he remains single throughout the series. A Mrs. Mayo is never mentioned. His cousin/housekeeper, Jenny, frequently serves as a comic foil to his detecting. In *Spring Harrowing*, Taylor describes Mayo for an article for *Newsorgan*, a mythical newsweekly magazine. "... tall, salty Cape Codder Asey Mayo. One-time sailor, mechanic, widely rotogravured as the Homespun Sleuth, Jack-of-All-Trades Mayo... Sleuth Mayo pioneered Porter Cars, made coast-to-coast tour in 1899 in two-cylindered Porter Century; drove Porter Bullet II in 1904 at Daytona Beach..."[3] Mayo has no end to his talents. After a few adventures, Mayo even gets a reputation for solving the mysterious crimes on the Cape. He is often referred to as the "Cod-

---

3. Phoebe Atwood Taylor, *Spring Harrowing* (New York: WW Norton & Co, 1939), page 6.

fish" Sherlock in some of the later books.

Taylor's creation is a far cry from the Golden Ages sleuths with their superhuman mental capacities. Mayo doesn't possess any special knowledge or intelligence. His methods are common sense and a knowledge of people. He doesn't fall for the murderer's elaborate schemes. His no-nonsense practicality serves him well. He shoots for the direct route and most often he is correct.

The Cape Cod Mystery's plot is fairly simple. Dale Sanborn, a well-known novelist, is discovered murdered in the cabin next to Prudence's summer home. The police quickly glom on to Bill Porter as the prime suspect. In an unusual turn of events, the local police don't have a jail to house Porter, so they keep him in pillory and in a boxcar in lieu of a real prison. In trying to locate the real killer, Mayo and Prudence learn that practically everyone in town (and a few weekend visitors) had a motive for Sanborn's death. The detecting duo have few clues to guide them, just a missing hammer and a sardine can.

Taylor had a knack for picking the oddest clues or "clews" as she spelled it in her books. Taylor blamed the spelling issue on a former teacher who had insisted on the old-fashioned spelling of the word. It was indicative of Taylor's nature to follow the established ways of the previous generations. With either spelling, the bizarre physical evidence added to the zaniness of the yarns. In *Spring Harrowing*, the clues included an old Porter Century car, a chess set, two wild bobcats, and a suit of armor. A lobster pot buoy is used as a murder weapon in *Proof of the Pudding*. In *Going, Going, Gone*, a set of bound magazines is a clue to the solution of the crimes. Taylor seemed to have a penchant for taking items from every day life and making them ominous. The items added to the ambience of the books, since many of the clues were highly specific to the New England region.

While murder is not a laughing matter, the detection process was fraught with humor in Taylor's works. Even beyond her collection of clues, Taylor's sense of humor is apparent. Bill Porter is an eccentric to begin with, prattling on to cover his true feelings for Prudence's niece. The lack of a jail cell adds humor to his rather dire situation. Mayo talks to him while Porter is hunched over in pillory with his hands and neck immobilized, like pre-Revolutionary punishment. The touch is awkwardly funny and yet indicative of the area, which places a premium on things past. Other characters are presented with an equally deft touch. Emma Manton is drawn rather "broadly" as a large woman who cannot move around without being heard, giving her an "ear-tight" alibi for the time of the murder. The maid is a taciturn woman who only speaks in monosyllables and hides the silverware for fear of theft whenever she leaves the summer home. All these touches bring a smile to the reader's face while the protagonists try to solve the crime.

Taylor's humor is not all directed at other people in her work. She even takes potshots at authors in her first book. She elaborated more on the subject in her Witherall books, but she couldn't resist a bit of tongue-in-cheek even at the beginning of her career. The victim in *The Cape Cod Mystery* is a writer who steals the plots of his literary novels from real life. Prudence reads detective novels and is forever commenting on the clues and the sleuth of the book she is reading. She thinks that Mayo selects her to help solve the murder because of her reading habits.

In today's mystery world, many series have a strong regional element, but in the years when Taylor was writing, most Golden Age authors set the story against a generic big city backdrop. A few authors wrote about specific metropolitan areas, but a Poirot or Wimsey mystery could exist anywhere in England, not just London. Not many series were so closely tied to a region as the Taylor series were. Asey Mayo or Leonidas Witherall could never prosper in the Midwest or the South in the same manner. When Taylor wove the regional traits of Cape Cod into the actual mystery, she was one of the first to do so, and remains one of the best.

The trend towards more regional flavor got a leg up from technology. The end of the twentieth century made remarkable progress toward globalization and as a result, the world found more and better ways to communicate. This boon in communication through e-mail, faxes, the Internet, cell phones made people better able to communicate with people in other parts of the country. These factors made New

York less of the publishing mecca. The decentralization of publishing through communications was one factor that has made regional mysteries a favorite of the second Golden Age.

While a few authors chose New England for a setting, many of the authors went further south for their crime scenes. One of the most popular regions of the country to experience a crime wave has been the South. For the most part, authors have shown America the eccentric ways of their Southern cousins. Even so, all areas from Alaska to West Virginia are now represented in mystery.

The second Golden Age has also seen a rise in the prevalence of humorous mysteries. While many people think that comedy is easy to write, a novel written for belly laughs is hard to find. After all, bad comedy can produce groans. What the author might find funny in the confines of his office while writing might leave the reader flat. Finding a universal appeal can be extremely difficult.

Comedy can come in many shapes. Puns are one form that has been used. Craig Rice used any number of puns as titles, and the trend continues today. Titles that are a play on words will clue in the reader to the funny contents of a book.

Comedy can also stem from circumstances and this was the type of humor most used by Taylor. A funny situation has the most universal appeal. The reader doesn't have to be literate to recognize a quote or a reference to make the joke work. If the character is jailed in a boxcar, the reader can see the fun in the situation.

Humor can also come from the character as well. The wise-cracking private eye or the sarcastic matron have a certain appeal, but the author has to walk a fine line between humor and mean-spiritedness. The humor in character is determined by the reader and a sensitive type might not think a sarcastic smart aleck to be amusing.

All types of comedic books are rarely recognized as having the same merit as more serious works. Indeed, although Taylor is one of the few authors in this book whose works are still in print, she did not receive the recognition from the Mystery Writers of America that the other authors did. She was never nominated for MWA's Edgar, nor did the organization bestow a Grand Master title upon her. Anthony

Boucher referred to her books as "farce melodramas", not recognizing her special talents as a comedic gift. While the critics might have been harsh, the fans found her works endearing. She is one of the few authors from the Cold War era who remains in print today.

Taylor did not waste any time in writing a follow-up to *The Cape Cod Mystery*. Her next book, *Death Lights a Candle*, appeared within the year. Taylor wrote quickly. Within four years, she had produced seven Asey Mayo novels. She spent most of her time at home nursing her aunt, corresponding with friends, and writing the mysteries. Within a few books, the first person narrator of *The Cape Cod Mystery* had transformed into a limited third person perspective following Mayo.

The cast of regular characters grew too. The supporting characters are well-drawn and typically Yankee in nature. Doc Cummings, the local GP, serves as sometimes Watson for Mayo, following around the sleuth and making the appropriate noises of appreciation. The doctor is probably best known for his inability to keep his patients in one place while the events of the book are in progress.

The local flavor is not limited to the characters. Even the happenings are New England in nature. In *Going, Going, Gone*, Taylor has Mayo find the corpse of a local woman found in a sea chest at an estate auction in Wellfleet. He makes his deductions based on what would have prevented the woman from attending the auction in the first place, as these sales were town happenings, like a fair or picnic.

> "Who cares about a little old piece of loose cane, when this genuine prewar aluminum pan is also offered! Thrown in! Why you can pick up a bit of cane and mend that seat in less than five minutes – but *where* can you find a genuine aluminum pan? The pessimist looks at the hole, ladies and gentlemen, but the optimist looks at the pan!"
>
> "Why, that's just exactly what Sharp *did* say!" Mrs. Turnover told him. "Were you there this afternoon, Mr. Mayo? I didn't see you."

"Nope, I wasn't there, but I been to other auctions."[4]

The vivid depiction of Cape Cod was not confined to the characters or the landscape. The weather is always represented in the books, just as Cape residents themselves note it. Plot points can turn on the tides, hurricanes that dredge up old shipwrecks, or snowstorms that prevent the characters from moving around. In *The Cape Cod Mystery*, a summer heat wave in New York and Boston give Prudence and her niece a number of weekend guests to choose from. Their selection ultimately becomes part of the mystery as the visitors are shown to have connections to the dead man.

Caring for her invalid aunt, Taylor couldn't get out of the house often. Her contact with the outside world was limited to Cape Cod and correspondence. She was an avid letter writer. Through her Asey Mayo books, Taylor struck up a friendship with Margaret Mitchell, author of *Gone with the Wind*. Mitchell was a huge fan of the Asey Mayo books and the two authors soon became friends. In one letter from 1943, Mitchell encourages the regionalism of Taylor's work. "I hope you put in a lot about Cape Cod background and people (and I don't care how damned quaint you make them because I don't have to spend my summers with them). I am convinced that over half the mystery fans read for background, color and character as well. So, for my money, and lots of other people's money, we can't have too much of the Cape."[5]

Beyond the regional flavor of the books, Taylor reflected the era in her details. The books set before the war deal with the hardships of the Great Depression. From 1941 to 1945, the reader gets a glimpse into the world of ration coupons that went on across the country, blackouts, people missing while serving at war. Taylor's fictional world is

---

4. Phoebe Atwood Taylor, *Going, Going, Gone* (New York: WW Norton & Co, 1943), page 115.
5. Letter from Margaret Mitchell to Phoebe Atwood Taylor, Boston University Special Collections, dated July 14, 1943.

such a mirror of the times that the reader can play historian and archaeologist as well as sleuth. This level of accuracy is leveraged well in the books. The reader is so entrenched in the minutiae of the book that it becomes easier to accept the more preposterous events that take place over the course of the novel. Were the book not so well grounded in real details, the reader might not be willing to move along with the plot.

These day-to-day particulars came easy to her as an author. Taylor was keenly aware of her own powers of observation. "I tell myself I don't see enough, but the photographic memory works in spite of myself and I notice as much as I do at home – the trick of observation is largely lost, I think, in childhood; I leaned to cover up long ago, but notice too much always, and it's helpful traveling, but if an occasional social curse at home."[6]

While Taylor produced 21 Mayo novels and two short novel collections in twenty years, she was not content to just write a single series. She wrote books under two other names as well, making her an extremely prodigious author for the times. In some years before the war, she would write as many as three books in a 12-month period.

Writing under the pseudonym of Alice Tilton, the name of her invalid aunt, Taylor developed a second series, featuring Leonidas Witherall. She wrote the majority of these books in the 1940s, ending the eight volume series after the end of World War II.

Witherall is a prep school teacher who pens fanciful mystery thrillers about the daring Lieutenant Haseltine and Lady Alicia under the pen name of Murgatroy Jones. Additionally, he is a dead ringer for William Shakespeare, which causes no end of difficulty for him in trying to solve these murders. He is frequently called "Bill" by the other characters in the books and of course, it is nearly impossible to forget his face once seen. "The resemblance was nothing short of uncanny. More than one Shakespeare lover had poked the midriff section of Leonidas Witherall with a tremulous forefinger to make sure the man was

---

6. Letter from Phoebe Atwood Taylor to Mrs. Elizabeth Manwaring, cousin, 1948, part of the Taylor collection at Boston University.

real. Even those to whom the Bard of Avon was at best a hazy memory were wont to stop short and wonder where in blazes they had seen that old duffer with the beard before. He looked so familiar."[7] His notoriety is only heightened by the number of people who recognize him from Meredith Academy.

The books take place in the fictional town of Dalton, a suburb of Boston, modeled on Newton where Taylor spent a great deal of time. While it wasn't her beloved Cape Cod, Taylor does a wonderful job of capturing the burgeoning Boston suburbs and details that make it unique. These works deal with new subdivisions, growing land development, and department stores that sprout up as people move away from city centers.

The books practically defy description. The books' elapsed time period is so abbreviated as to feel harried. Rarely does a book take more than 48 hours for Witherall to solve the crime. There are always reasons for working around the clock to solve the crime. In one book, Witherall wants to solve the crime between a Friday and Monday so that the police will release the young man they arrested for the crime. In other cases, some event at Meredith Academy dictates that he solve the crime as soon as possible to reduce the chances of the school suffering for Witherall's excursions into crime. To his chagrin, Witherall is the primary suspect in at least half of the cases, with the corpse appearing at his house or in a place where he was the last one to visit the deceased.

The openings are always a surprise to the reader. Taylor never bothered with a slow build-up to a situation in this series. The books open with immediate action. In *Dead Ernest*, two strangers in a red truck deliver a deep freeze chest to his house with the body of the French schoolteacher inside. In *File For Record*, he is knocked unconscious in Haymaker's Department Store while in the Lost and Found department and wakes up on a bread truck heading out of town. In *The Cut Direct*, Witherall wakes up under a parked car on a dark street with

---

7. Phoebe Atwood Taylor writing as Alice Tilton, *Beginning With a Bash* (New York: WW Norton & Co, 1937), page 7.

no idea how he got there. In *Cold Steal*, Witherall returns from an around-the-world trip to find a dead body in his home.

Even under a pseudonym, the books share a number of traits with those written under Taylor's given name. Similar to the Mayo series, the clues are unique and varied as the series was. In *The Iron Clew*, items left at the crime scene include a brick of cheese, a monkey, Pistachio ice cream, and a mink coat. Only someone with Taylor's imagination and talent could weave all of these clues into a satisfying solution in 200 pages.

The humor in the Witherall series is more pronounced and defined than that of the Mayo series. The situations border on the preposterous. The clues are fanciful and the pace of the books set a land speed record. Not many authors can glibly fling about the wit and humor like Taylor did. The books are mad-capped in nature, slapstick, and fun. Even though these are murders, robberies, and assaults, in very few instances do the crimes dampen the frivolous nature of the books.

Even if she did not find critical success, the comedy allowed her more leeway than many other writers of the time. Taylor was able to plant her tongue firmly in her cheek using the Witherall series, making the hero the author of the Lieutenant Haseltine adventure series under a pen name. In this manner, she related to the readers some of the difficulties in writing a series of novels, especially under a pen name. People assumed that Witherall was as brave, noble and ingenious as his character. Witherall would distill the adventures he had just endured into his next Haseltine novel, so that the reader knew something of the fictional series as well reading an intriguing mystery.

Fans should note that Taylor wrote her books much as Witherall did his. Witherall has trouble in finding time to write and cranked out books at a remarkable speed to meet a deadline. Likewise, Taylor started a new mystery about three weeks before the deadline for the finished manuscript and worked her best from midnight to three A.M. most days. On one manuscript, she scribbled, "Phoebe has written one book in fifteen days and does not care to repeat the process." *Banbury Bog* was written in twenty days. Before the age of computerized cut and paste, Taylor would write sixty thousand words, revise it, make sure that all the plot points were covered, and retype it in a matter of less than a month. In another letter she relates her strategy for writing the fast-paced adventures. "I know there's nothing now but for me to get down to the business of writing; only it seems – well there's no point in disillusioning you, but my scripts usually reach people on time, via air express. They've never been known to reach anyone ahead of time, ever. It's all on account of my habit of not beginning a script until two weeks before it is due. Then the suspense, you see, is genuine... [Y]ou can't murder slowly"[8] She followed her own advice, managing to sometimes write two or three books per year. Her advice to most new authors was to stick to the story line and not veer off into extraneous matters.

While she was writing two series, Bennett Cerf of Random House approached Taylor in 1938. He wanted a mystery novel that would take place at the 1939 New York World's Fair. However, he wanted the book to be published prior to the fair for the sake of advance publicity. Taylor agreed to write *Murder at the New York World's Fair*, under a second pen name of Freeman Dana, another concoction from her family history. She toured the fair site in Flushing Meadows, New York, in April of 1938 and then set to work. Taylor had to use her active imagination, because the fair site was nothing more than muddy fields when she began to write the book. She surrounded herself with publicity materials, architectural renderings of the buildings and a map of the fair site. In 31 days, she had finished a first draft of the novel.

The book suffered a number of editorial revisions, something that Taylor was not used to. She chafed a bit under the direction and the correspondence between author and editor was less than pleasant. The book was published in November 1938 with a first printing of just 900 copies. Taylor considered the book so insignificant that she didn't even bother to list it in her credentials.

By the end of World War II, Taylor was tiring of the phenom-

---

8. Freeman Dana, *Murder at the New York's World Fair (New York:* Random House, 1938), afterward by Ellen Nehr.

enal pace she'd been keeping. Not only was the writing exhausting, she found it difficult to concoct new plots for her sleuths. In the final Witherall mystery, *The Iron Clew*, Taylor summed up the difficulty in writing a series that bridged the Depression, world war, and the atomic age. "... 'Consider, Mrs. Mullet, how thwarting this brave new world is to a character like the fiery Lieutenant Haseltine. Take the–er–achievement of Atomic Power, on which I've relied so often for plots in the past—you know,' he went on explanatorily, 'some sinister foreign government would be about to loose some infernal atomic machine on the world, and Haseltine, with the aid of the Lady Alicia and Faithful Frank, somehow ferreted out the diabolical details, grabbed The Thing in the nick of time, and saved humanity from for yet another volume. But now that The Thing actually exists, I can't use it... all are passé, Mrs. Mullet. Old hat, in a nutshell... We're Good Neighbors,' he said with a sigh, 'and this is One World. No, I've tramped this room for miles, brooding vigorously every inch of the way, and I can conjure up nothing from which Haseltine can rescue Lady Alicia and humanity. Absolutely nothing. In one hundred and seven volumes, the gallant lieutenant has never before been forced to cope with the simple toys of peace."[9] The reader could almost imagine that Taylor was talking for herself in the matter.

Her post-war output declined rapidly. She went from writing two to three books a year to less than one per year. Her aunt had passed away during the war and Taylor found herself free to tour the country and the world. She wasted no time in escaping from the Cape where she had grown up and lived for the past 15 years. She spent a great part of 1948 traveling Europe with friends. Her letters back to the U.S. present that same pragmatic New Englander that she shows throughout her series. "The English know less of us than of anyone. It's impossible for them grasp beyond county borders. They can't see U.S. in miles. 'I dare says it's quite vast and rustic. I shouldn't like it.' No sense of on-with-job, as to get done. Sluggers. Insular. Prejudicial.

---

9. Phoebe Atwood Taylor writing as Alice Tilton, *The Iron Clew* (New York: WW Norton & Co, 1947), page 9.

Tired. Occupied countries have bounced back quicker."[10] After a summer of travel, Taylor was ready to return to the Unites States and its creature comforts.

Not long after her return from Europe, Taylor changed her life yet again. In 1951, she married Dr. Grantly Walden Taylor, a Boston surgeon, having the common sense to marry a man with the same last name as her own. Taylor had waited until her aunt's passing and a tour of the world before settling down. She was 42. Within the year, she had given up writing for good. She was adamant in her decision to retire. After twenty years of writing two of the most popular series of her times, she chose to quit when she married.

Taylor did not leave much in the way of personal data for future biographers. She was too old to have children by the time of her marriage and so the Taylor heritage went no further. Beyond a few personal letters and marked-up manuscripts, little is known about the world of her writing, due to the insular nature of her life with her aunt. Indeed, the archivists at Boston University did not have information about literary executors for her estate. According to Dr. Howard B. Gotlieb, former Director of Special Collections at Boston University, "I could not reach past her social politeness. Authors often love to talk about themselves of their writing, but I felt a slight reserve or remoteness about Taylor." [11]

Taylor was true to her word of not writing again and passed away on January 9, 1976.

---

10. Letter from Phoebe Atwood Taylor to Mrs. WP White, dated August 23, 1948, part of the Taylor collection at Boston University.

11. Katherine Kominis "Never Out of Style: Phoebe Atwood Taylor", *Firsts Magazine*, (November 1991): page 22.

Similar Authors Published Today:

- Charlotte Macleod
- Deborah Adams
- Joan Hess
- Margaret Maron
- Taylor McCafferty

Bibliography

As Phoebe Atwood Taylor

The Cape Cod Mystery - - - - - - - - - - -1931
Death Lights a Candle - - - - - - - - - - -1932
The Mystery of the Cape Cod Players - - -1933
The Mystery of the Cape Cod Tavern - - -1934
Sandbar Sinister - - - - - - - - - - - - -1934
Deathblow Hill - - - - - - - - - - - - - -1935
The Tinkling Symbol - - - - - - - - - - -1935
The Crimson Patch - - - - - - - - - - - -1936
Out of Order - - - - - - - - - - - - - - -1936
Figure Away - - - - - - - - - - - - - - -1937
Octagon House - - - - - - - - - - - - - -1937
The Annulet of Gilt - - - - - - - - - - - -1938
Banbury Bog - - - - - - - - - - - - - - -1938
Spring Harrowing - - - - - - - - - - - - -1939
The Criminal C.O.D. - - - - - - - - - - -1940
The Deadly Sunshade - - - - - - - - - - -1940
The Perennial Boarder - - - - - - - - - - -1941
The Six Iron Spiders - - - - - - - - - - -1942
Three Plots for Asey Mayo - - - - - - - -1942
Going, Going, Gone - - - - - - - - - - - -1943
Asey Mayo Trio - - - - - - - - - - - - -1943
Proof of the Pudding - - - - - - - - - - -1945
Punch with Care - - - - - - - - - - - - -1946
Diplomatic Corpse - - - - - - - - - - - -1951

As Alice Tilton

Beginning with a Bash - - - - - - - - - -1937
The Cut Direct - - - - - - - - - - - - - -1938
Cold Steal - - - - - - - - - - - - - - - -1939
The Left Leg - - - - - - - - - - - - - - -1940
The Hollow Chest - - - - - - - - - - - - -1941
File for Record - - - - - - - - - - - - - -1943
Dead Ernest - - - - - - - - - - - - - - -1944
The Iron Clew - - - - - - - - - - - - - -1947

As Dana Freeman

Murder at the New York World's Fair - - -1939

CHAPTER 4 -- Dorothy B. Hughes

The term "renaissance author" might have been coined for Dorothy B. Hughes. Not only did she write suspense novels, she reviewed the works of other mystery authors for four decades and completed the definitive biography of the frenetic life of Erle Stanley Gardner, the creator of Perry Mason. Outside of the genre, she wrote poetry and general non-fiction about her beloved Southwest.

Born Dorothy Belle Flanagan in Kansas City, Missouri, in 1904, she had a desire to write from the earliest age. In 1925, Dorothy graduated from the University of Missouri with a journalism degree. She worked for a time at the *Kansas City Journal* before moving to New York to further her writing career. She did graduate work at Columbia University in New York City while writing for the area newspapers.

While living in New York, Hughes traveled to Santa Fe to help her pregnant sister. She loved the area so much that she chose to stay. She transferred her credits from Columbia to the University of New Mexico working toward a Masters in English. She supported herself by teaching Basic English classes, working in journalism to make ends meet. Her sister and brother-in-law both wrote for the local paper. They provided the contacts for Dorothy to find work.

In 1930, she met Levi Hughes while attending a wedding reception. The couple married in 1932 and eight months later Hughes bore her first child, Holly. Hughes returned to Kansas City to have the baby, but quickly returned to the Southwest. Hughes lived in Albuquerque for a short stint, but moved back to Santa Fe to be closer to her sister and her husband's family.

Even before her marriage, Dorothy began to prove her literary versatility. Her graduate program required courses in poetry. Encouraged by her peers and professors, she published a book of poems, *Dark Certainty*. Well received, the book was named one of the Yale Series of Younger Poets in 1931. Hughes loved poetry, and its intense concentration on language, but poetry didn't pay enough to help support her.

Hughes followed her poetry collection with *Pueblo on the Mesa: The First Fifty Years of the University of New Mexico* in 1939. The book reflected Hughes love of the Southwest, which she made her home. New Mexico's literary scene at the time was thriving. During her stay in Santa Fe, she met literary figures like D. H. Lawrence and T. S. Eliot.

Hughes also wanted to try her hand at fiction. For years, she had wanted to write a mystery novel, a classic whodunit, without success. Exasperated, she read the work of Graham Greene and realized the quality of his characterization. She decided to write a novel of characters that included a crime and tension as well. "I thought I am going to write one that really has literary quality, forget about doing mystery, you just have that suspense."[1] Characterization became paramount to the book reviews she began to write about this time. Hughes harped on the need for "real" people in mysteries. She gave preference to novels with a strong lead character who grew from the book's experiences.

1. Oral History Interview with Dorothy B. Hughes. Center for Southwest Research, General Library, University of New Mexico.

Armed with her new insights into writing mysteries, Hughes' first mystery novel appeared in 1940. *The So Blue Marble* is the story of a small blue marble that holds the secrets to a lost civilization. While the plot is far-fetched, the stone's powers are only obliquely explained in the book. The main thrust of the novel is the terror that could exist under the seemingly shallow façade of Manhattan's cocktail set. The people who produced the marble were said to have harnessed the sun in new ways as well as the forces of gravity, giving man total dominion over the earth. The stone also provides a map for colossal gems and riches. However, like many precious gems, the marble has a long history of death and bloodshed.

The book's main character, Griselda, is a divorced movie actress and fashion designer visiting New York City. She becomes trapped between factions who want to control the marble and its powers. The valuable stone belonged to Griselda's ex-husband who has taken a job reporting on a border problem outside the city. The book opens powerfully as two unknown men take Griselda by each arm and escort her back to her apartment for a late night drink. The seemingly innocent social scene is fraught with tension.

Griselda doesn't know whom to trust as she tries to learn what the marble means. "There was no place for her to go, no place to lie her head. Suppose Inspector Tobin had taken her away in that car. Suppose the twins should close in on her now, or Missy, with a hatchet in her hand. Gig might take her, lock her in again. The panic that had been here all day surged now unbearably. She'd have to hide away to stay safe for Con. Other people hid in New York. She would go to a hotel. But she wanted her own things, a change of clothes. It was reckless, but it should be perfectly safe now,"[2]

The book also contains a quasi-romance between Griselda and her ex-husband, Con. She had written a letter to Con explaining her quest to protect the marble. The letter also told Con how much she still loves him. Griselda goes to great lengths to try to keep the letter from

---

2. Hughes, Dorothy B. *The So Blue Marble*, Duell, Sloan, and Pearce (New York, 1940), page 154.

him until the last possible moment, when a reconciliation is effected between the estranged couple. Despite the rather improbable relationship, the book received wide-spread and immediate acclaim from the critics.

Not only would Hughes go on to write 11 highly acclaimed novels, she also read and reviewed mysteries for publications around the country. From 1940 to 1979, Hughes worked as a respected mystery reviewer for the *Albuquerque Tribune, Los Angeles Times, New York Herald-Tribune* and other newspapers. She fondly remembered spending many an afternoon in California, discussing books and reviews with Anthony Boucher (who would later become the mystery reviewer for *The New York Times*) and Craig Rice who reviewed books for fun. While Hughes never reviewed her own novels, she did list the novels of her friends and colleagues in her columns.

Despite the lead of friends like Ellery Queen and Erle Stanley Gardner, Hughes recognized that she couldn't have a series character. "It didn't work for me. I tried one time and couldn't have the same character."[3] So she followed *The So Blue Marble* with *The Bamboo Blonde*, and then *The Fallen Sparrow*, one of her best-known works. *The Fallen Sparrow*, written during World War II, was dedicated to Eric Ambler who had "no book this year." Ambler was off fighting for Britain, obviously unable to write. Just as women picked up the slack on the home front, Hughes managed to fill in for the author soldiers in the spy novel market. She did a remarkable job of penning an espionage book, though the patriotism gets a bit thick at times.

The book revolves around the life of a Spanish Civil War veteran who comes home only to relive experiences similar to his POW incarceration. Kit McKittrick returns to New York City after spending years in a Spanish prisoner of war camp. He was held long after most other prisoners were released because he possessed a collection of rare goblets coveted by his captors.

---

3. Oral History Interview with Dorothy B. Hughes. Center for Southwest Research, General Library, University of New Mexico.

When a weakened and wary Kit returns to New York City, he finds that the man who helped him escape has been murdered. For the first half of the book, the reader is unsure of Kit's sanity — whether or not the murder stems from delusions brought on by his captivity or if his suspicious nature is correct. The growing tension comes from the easy way that the police are able to explain away his fears and suspicions.

While he trusts no one, Kit is especially distrusting of the refugees who came to America to escape Hitler. Many of these expatriates reside with the families of his friends, without identification or social introductions. The lack of social references makes it easy to infiltrate the tight-knit society group in which Kit marginally participates. New York City is portrayed as a city in flux, chaotic and without moorings. The recurring theme of an outsider taking on figures representing social institutions is repeated in most all of Hughes' works. The upper class milieu of the book adds to the unreality of the situation as Kit has access to the hoi polloi through his stepfather.

While staying with his mother and upper class stepfather, Kit begins to suspect that he was released from his prison camp. Although he had technically escaped, he wonders if his captors had released him subtly in order to find the lost goblets. The reader begins to question if the years in solitary have taken a toll on Kit as he sees mysterious men go into buildings never to be seen again. Kit crashes parties and visits acquaintenances in the middle of the night, making him seem erratic and unstable. The police and his friends don't believe that his friend who helped him escape was murdered. The police feel that the death was an unfortunate accident. In an amusing twist for the readers, the police investigator is Inspector Tobin, who appeared in *The So Blue Marble*.

The story moves quickly as Kit begins to hear footstep in New York, similar to those he heard in the prisoner camp. The mysterious footsteps that he attributes to a man he calls "Wobblefoot" are heard in the unlikely big city environs. Kit has never seen the man, though he heard the man's unique footsteps on a monthly basis while in prison.

Kit only trusts the family of his dead friend, until he begins to piece the puzzle together. He gets a cab assigned to him by his friends so as not to worry about ambush from the mysterious people he fears. The work ends with a wonderful twist that provides closure to the story.

Hughes' fame grew immensely when the book was made into a movie starring John Garfield in 1943. "I got John Garfield who was very tops in those days and Maureen O'Hara who was new and a beautiful actress! I had all these stars in it and I had production values that befitted what they called an 'A' performer. I had nothing whatever to do with it."[4]

Hughes visited the set during filming of *The Fallen Sparrow*, one of many trips across America for the author. Hughes moved constantly during her career. From Missouri, she went to New York, Texas, New Mexico, Arizona, California and more. Reflecting the constant state of motion in her own life, one of Hughes' books was set on a cross-country train. *Dread Journey* takes place on a train traveling from Los Angeles to Chicago with a motley cast of characters. Kitten Agnew, a Hollywood starlet, is frightened for her life as she prepares to mount a legal battle against her producer, Vivien Spender. She and Spender had been lovers before a very recent and public split, caused by Spender finding a new girlfriend, Gratia Shawn, who is also a passenger on the train. The cast is rounded out by Spender's longtime personal assistant, a screenwriter fired from Spender's studio, a frightened musician, and a burned-out writer who has seen too much death at the front lines of the war.

In the first sentence of the book, Kitten sums up the situation. She is afraid of Spender. He's a megalomaniac who is used to getting his way and only sees things from his perspective. For Kitten to oppose him in firing her from his latest effort, a long-desired telling of a particular biography, she risks Spender's wrath and her own life. Spender murdered his first wife and he plans to kill Kitten in the same

4. Oral History Interview with Dorothy B. Hughes. Center for Southwest Research, General Library, University of New Mexico.

manner, despite the growing realization of his intentions by others. Kitten stands firm in her desire to have the part and has accumulated incriminating documents that would ruin Spender if she released them.

While technically a novel of suspense, the book has little mystery. The killer and victim are identified in the first pages. The method of murder is vague, but provided to the reader as well. The source of tension comes not from whodunit, but "will he do it?" The action comes from Kitten's and Spender's cat-and-mouse game of murder. Kitten refuses appointments made by Spender, and Spender remains in his compartment for much of the journey for fear of being publicly linked to his new amour. The pair tries to outmaneuver and one-up each other until a fateful meeting between the two characters, about two-thirds of the way through the book.

Short segments in the narration told from the point of view of a young honeymooning couple and Cobbett, a black Pullman car attendant, punctuate the taut suspense of the novel. The attendant's actions and thoughts are far removed from the life and death struggle going on under his eye. He helps move the plot forward, but also gives a counterpoint to remind the reader that the world goes on, even as someone is murdered. The daily routine also delineates the rather trivial beginnings of the impetus to murder. The crime is about the desire to play a particular part in a movie, a role in a fantasy.

Hughes followed *Dread Journey* with another taut suspense novel. Hughes' first post-war book was *Ride the Pink Horse*, a thriller set in New Mexico. The title refers to the carousel owned by Pancho, one of the main characters in the book. When Sailor, the book's protagonist buys a ride for one of the local girls, he insists that she ride the pink horse, a rather whimsical and feminine color for a girl who has little need of either in her life.

Sailor has come to Santa Fe to collect a debt owed to him by a former Senator who is also his former employer. The annual Fiesta is in progress and the town is crowded. Sailor can't find lodging in town and has to make do with the local merry-go-round ride operator's floor. Despite the hordes of people in town for the event, Sailor continues to run into the same people repeatedly: the Senator; the ride operator; a detective named McIntyre who is on the trail of the Senator; and a young girl named Pila.

Again with Hughes' deft touch the carousel becomes a metaphor for a person's life. Despite the difference in how their lives have turned out, Sailor and McIntyre, the detective, share a common past. They both grew up in the same underprivileged neighborhood and faced the same lack of opportunities. Yet McIntyre is the head of the Homicide division in Chicago while Sailor is a grifter who wants payment for a debt owed to him by a corrupt ex-Senator. Sailor has put himself on a path with no way off (like a carousel) and no good conclusion. McIntyre explains, "The world doesn't care much what happens to us. Least that's the way I've always figured. Like this table... it doesn't care if you bump your shin on it. It doesn't even know if you're around. That's the world. The I way I see it... It's up to you what you are. Good or bad. You get the choice. You can do anything you want to with yourself... The only way I can see it is that maybe God doesn't want those that choose the devil. He withholds His hand, waits for them to turn to Him."[5]

Similarly, the young girl that Sailor befriends rides the carousel in the one scene. She is supposed to be out prowling for a man to seduce for spending money, but instead Sailor buys her a meal and gives the girl money for the carnival ride. The girl gets a momentary taste of a childhood she will never have; she has to go back to her shanty life at the end of the story. Sailor realizes that he can fulfill a few of her dreams and spends his last dollars to buy her a home permanent.

Hughes also uses the book to discuss the subject of class and caste in the United States after the war. Based on social status, the characters in the book stay in different hotels and Sailor has to steer his way between the different establishments. He's extremely conscious of his recent decline from Senator's aide to unemployed drifter. The social scale is presented most clearly in the treatment of Mexicans

---

5. Hughes, Dorothy B. *Ride the Pink Horse*, William Morrow and Company (New York, 1946), pages 105-106.

in the book. The whites look down on the Mexicans as all one race, but internally, the Mexicans of Spanish descent look down upon the Mexican Indians. Sadly, Pila is an Indian in a family of Spaniards who treat her as an outcast. Throughout the book, Sailor calls the carousel operator Pancho, in reference to Pancho Villa, a derogatory reference to his race. His attitude persists even though the operator is the only man Sailor feels he can trust in Santa Fe. When he tries later in the book to find the man, he realizes that he doesn't even know the man's real name.

Sailor is the navigator between the social classes. He is too familiar with the way society treats him. He is careful to only appear at La Fonda, the swanky hotel, after he has cleaned up. He fears being looked down upon by the staff. He has studied the ways to re-invent himself as more refined, even though his childhood was poverty-ridden. His descent again into the lower classes is a reminder of how fast things can change. With the Fiesta in town, he is suddenly forced out of doors and sleeps on the ground under the carousel operator's shawl.

Hughes' vision of the post-war years was not the manor house and aristocracy of the 1930s. She portrayed a much seedier version of cities and the new suburbia. She painted bleak sketches of the hypocrisy of the new middle class who wanted privacy from their neighbors at the same time they wanted the close quarters of planned communities and high-rise apartment buildings.

Ride the Pink Horse was optioned by Hollywood and made into a film. "Bob Montgomery bought that for his release through Universal, but though his own production company and I think he directed that and Joan Harrison who was Hitchcock's right hand woman, she produced it and I worked for his company for a period too, which is rather funny."[6] Montgomery, who had created a little New Mexico in the backlot for his purposes, invited Hughes to the set. The merry-go-round had been imported from Taos, brought to Hollywood on a flat-

6. Oral History Interview with Dorothy B. Hughes. Center for Southwest Research, General Library, University of New Mexico.

bed truck. While the scenes were not authentic, it was close enough to please Hughes.

The sale of a second novel to Hollywood caused Hughes and her young brood to move to Los Angeles. Levi Hughes left his work in the oil business to join his family's firm. His new job allowed him to work more from home with occasional trips to Santa Fe and Cleveland. Hughes sent her sister ahead to scout out places to live in L.A. as she was raising three small children by now. Ironically, Hughes' next book, *The Blackbirder*, was not optioned to be a film.

The Blackbirder tells of Julie Marlebone, a French ex-patriate who has snuck into the United States after the fall of France to the Nazis. Julie tried to keep a very low profile because her adopted uncle, a Frenchman who sided with the Nazis to help conquer France, is hunting her. She absconded from the country with a priceless family heirloom and possession of the family fortune. When an acquaintance from her time in Paris bumps into her in New York City and is shot minutes after the encounter, Julie starts a cross-country journey to escape the killers and to free her cousin and first love, Fran, from jail. She wants to use an illegal freight plane, called the Blackbirder, to flee to Mexico and evade the law and her pursuers. At one point, Julie hides from the police in the home of a group of Indians. The lower class is the only place she can find sanctuary.

Even before it became a major theme in her work, Hughes was a proponent for racial equality. Her husband's family had not shown bias to the Mexicans and Indians in New Mexico and she learned from their ways. In Hollywood, she would frequently invite black friends out to swanky restaurants in order to try to provoke a scene. More often than not, the staff would just serve the group, making for an informal integration.

Hughes is probably best known for her next book, *In a Lonely Place*. The book was later made into a Humphrey Bogart vehicle with Gloria Grahame, and directed by Nicholas Ray. The 1950 movie became a noir classic, in the dark vein of the James M. Cain movies. The book also foretold the McCarthy era with Hughes' depiction of screenwriters as a new breed of worker who are trapped by Hollywood's greed and star system.

The book is even darker than the movie. Dix Steele is a writer in name only. He uses the creative profession to gain an entrance to polite society. His good looks and charm mask a calculating mind and uncontrolled rage.

In a Lonely Place is characteristic of many of Hughes' works. Even the title indicates the solitary, isolated nature of her protagonists. These are not men who participate in the day-to-day mechanics of society. Her protagonists are men who live on the outskirts of society. While they may live in the suburbs with thousands of neighbors, they are separated from other people due to secrets and lies. The characters are flawed in ways that make them isolated.

Every aspect of Steele's life emphasizes his loneliness. His living arrangement causes him to be apart. Steele sublets a place from a college pal who has gone to Rio for a yearlong job assignment. Steele knows no one in the area and with no set schedule or employment; his socializing is minimal at best.

Additionally, writing can never be called a social profession. It involves long periods of time alone with just a typewriter and white paper. While his Uncle Fergus had agreed to finance a year's income for Steele, the reader never sees the character involved in any part of the writing process. In fact, the proposed novel continues to change form as the book progresses, from serious literature to murder mystery.

In many of the books Hughes wrote just after World War II, the protagonists are soldiers home from the front. These men return from the war troubled. Dix Steele had found his niche as a flyboy in England, but was forced to return to America to attempt to fit into society again. "The war years were the first happy years he'd ever known. You didn't have to kowtow to the stinking rich, you were all equal in pay; and before long you were the rich guy. Because you didn't give a damn and you were the best God-damned pilot in the company with promotions coming fast. You wore swell tailored uniforms, high polish on your shoes... That life was so real that there wasn't any other life. Even when the war was over there was no realization of another life."[7] Overseas, Steele had a taste of a life that would end with VE day along with a taste for killing and risks.

In a Lonely Place has a relatively simple plot. After the war, Dix Steele has moved to Los Angeles to write. He decides to look up his old friend, Brub, while he's there. Brub is now a policeman, working on a serial killer case regarding young women strangled by a charming stranger. Because of the insight into Steele's character, it is soon apparent that he is the strangler who has been attacking young women. Like his hard surname, he shows no remorse for the crimes. He methodically reads the newspapers for confirmation that his prey has been found and he gets a morbid satisfaction after learning details about the women from the news articles.

Steele's relationships to women are very problematic. His attitude towards Brub's wife, Sylvia, varies widely through the course of the book. He moves from distrust and a certain anger at her to a level of desire for the woman and then anger and distrust as the noose starts to tighten around his neck.

Likewise, his relationship to his quasi-girlfriend, Lauren, is troubling. He meets the woman at his apartment complex and decides to fall for her even before they meet. His emotions are chosen, not experienced. His passion for her is frightening as he waits for her to stop by on the day after their first date. His ardor for this woman is almost matched by his annoyance with most other women. When meeting Brub's friends, Steele immediately is repulsed by the wife of one couple and wants nothing more than to silence her forever. "He took a deep breath outside to expel the odor of Maude from his lungs. He'd like to meet her on a dark corner. It would be a service to humanity."[8] Steele has no middle ground in his relationships with women.

These unsatisfying relationships only serve to highlight

7. Hughes, Dorothy B. *In a Lonely Place*, William Morrow and Company (New York, 1947), page 111.

8. Hughes, Dorothy B. *In a Lonely Place*, William Morrow and Company (New York, 1947), page 51.

Steele's apartness from those around him. He plans his life like a chess game, each move part of a bigger strategy. He stalks his prey at night, calculated so no one is around. He meets women as part of a well-planned pick-up scenario. The shallow meetings are his sole interactions with the residents of Los Angeles except for his friendship with Brub. His only daily routine is to leave the house so as to not see the cleaning service and to read the papers for information about his latest kill.

Hughes captured the tense time in Los Angeles after the war, even as they affected her own life. After World War II, Hollywood was fraught with fear over accusations of Communism in the ranks. Just before the time of McCarthy, Hollywood started to police its own. Through her work in the Screenwriters Guild and the Author's Guild, Hughes came under fire for her part in clearing many of the writers she had worked with over the years. That was not what many witchhunters at the time wanted to hear. Hughes was sympathetic to many of the accused and knew them to be good people who had merely associated with Communists. Hughes found herself blacklisted from writing for Hollywood again. "I didn't get another assignment. I didn't care. I was writing books. I made more money writing books and got more, good money out there. I never did anything about it."[9]

Even though she stopped writing for the movies, she continued her mystery reviews. Hughes, who received the Edgar for her reviews and criticism in 1950, added prestige to the genre by holding books to the same high standards of literary novels. Reviews and well-received biographies lent an air of respectability to what had been considered "popular" fiction. Many mysteries were relegated to a second-class status as paperback novels that were only considered a good beach read. No thought-provoking message could come from genre fiction.

At the time of Hughes' interest in literary critique of the genre, only the lives of a few of the major practitioners had been recorded.

9. Oral History Interview with Dorothy B. Hughes. Center for Southwest Research, General Library, University of New Mexico.

Sir Arthur Conan Doyle had been profiled, but even leaders in the field like Agatha Christie had not been studied. Hughes' reviews helped to open the door for other biographies and books about the field. The second Golden Age includes a healthy review of the books and authors who came before.

The scholarly work done for mystery fiction provided respectability. If a novel is good enough to be considered seriously, then it is important enough to review and study. The second Golden Age has seen a strong increase in the teaching of mystery fiction at the college level, something that would have been unheard of in 1950. Some of Hughes' work aided in elevating mystery to its place as a legitimate literary form.

Even though Hughes' novels are dark affairs, she had the versatility to write a much lighter mystery. She wrote a Sherlock Holmes pastiche entitled "Sherlock Holmes and the Muffin" about one of Mrs. Hudson's servants at 221B Baker Street. Hughes' ample research into the genre make these flights of fancy an easy task to complete. The story was lighthearted and amusing with a spunky heroine who is as perceptive and brave as Holmes.

Though she moved into short stories, Hughes continued to write novels as well. Published in 1950, *The Candy Kid* tells the story of Jose Aragon, a well-to-do Mexican who is mistaken by a mysterious blonde woman for a migrant worker. Most of the action in the book takes place in El Paso, Texas and features a mix of whites, Mexicans, and Spanish people. The blonde hires Aragon to pick up a package in Juarez from the local crime lord and deliver it to Santa Fe. After Aragon retrieves the package, a young girl from Juarez, who is owned by the crime lord, steals it. Aragon must locate the package again and find out why so many people are following him for the contents. In another tie-in from earlier books, the rendezvous is scheduled to take place at La Fonda, the same hotel that the Senator stayed in during *Ride the Pink Horse*.

While the reader expects that Aragon will end up with the beautiful blonde, it soon becomes obvious that this will not happen. The title references the blonde's name, which is Dulcinda. The Spanish word for candy is Dulce, which also serves as the woman's nickname. The romantic elements of the book continue to throw the reader off-balance as the expected relationships do not develop as the plot builds to a deadly ending.

Without making a point of it, Hughes studies the effects of racism in the book. The blonde assumes that Aragon is a migrant worker since he is Mexican; therefore, she has no compunction about hiring him for a potentially lethal assignment. The implications are that the itinerant farmer's life is less valuable than that of the Anglo tourists. In addition, Dulcinda does not expect a great deal of intelligence out of him, assuming he is uneducated. Even after she discovers her error, she holds certain racial stereotypes about the man that she does nothing to correct.

The Davidian Report followed *The Candy Kid*. Davidian is a former resident of Berlin who has copied and memorized sensitive information regarding the communist regime in Germany after the war. Stefan Winterich, a political operative, has been hired by the Communists to hunt down Davidian, get the report, and eliminate Davidian. Because of fog, Steve's plane to LAX is delayed and Steve's contact is murdered at LA's airport while they are waiting to land. The loss of his contact means that Steve has to retrace much of the same ground. He quickly learns that Davidian is hiding somewhere in the Hollywood area. The missing man is a sharp forger who leaves fake rubles as a calling card at the places he visits. Davidian has too many years of trying to stay alive to be caught easily, though he trusts Steve and wants to work with him for a solution to the papers he has stolen.

Steve meets up with a former flame, Janni, who is now satisfied with her new life in America. She had been a starving dancer in Berlin after the fall of Germany. She knows where Davidian is and how to contact him. Steve has to play on her affections to pry the information out of her. She tries to persuade Steve to stop his quest for the papers and settle down with her in Los Angeles. A young soldier named Rueben, or Rube for short, who may be working for the F.B.I, hampers Steve in his efforts.

In stark contrast to the Hollywood of actors and producers shown in *Dread Journey*, Hughes presents a bleak view of Hollywood, a place of boarding houses, wannabe actors, and Communist meeting places. Even in a place of fantasy, the reality can be dark and gloomy. Most of these characters live on the edge of poverty with little hope of the reknown Hollywood glamor.

Like many of her early works, Hughes presents a decadent upper class that lacks the moral passion of the people who are after the report for political reasons. Feather, the socialite who hooks up with Steve and Rueben, is looking for excitement rather than commitment to a political cause. While she can be quite dangerous, her only cause is her own fulfillment.

After *The Davidian Report*, Hughes took an eleven-year hiatus from writing novels. She continued to review books and write short stories for magazines such as *Ellery Queen's Mystery Magazine* and *Cosmopolitan*. In many of the stories, Hughes takes up the banner of minorities. Her works are filled with the Spanish and Mexicans of the Southwest United States and blacks across the country. In her sparse dark style, she depicted societal ills without lecturing or preaching about what should be done. The people were treated in such a way as to take prejudice to its logical conclusion.

Her next novel was equally shocking and socially motivated. She won her second Edgar in 1963 for *The Expendable Man*, a different story of social injustice. In *The Expendable Man*, the protagonist is painted as slightly paranoid in the early pages of the book, but no explanation is given. Dr. Hugh Densmore drives his parents' Cadillac from Los Angeles to Phoenix. He picks up a possibly underage and penniless female hitchhiker. He tries to send her home on a few separate occasions, but she continues to cross his path. She cashes in a bus ticket back to L.A. that he gave her in order to continue her trek to Phoenix. When a girl with similar features is found murdered, Densmore becomes a suspect. It isn't until the police question Densmore that the reader learns that the protagonist is black. This occurs some 50 pages into the book and radically changes the perception of the events that had taken place up to this point in the story.

Following her second Edgar for *The Expendable Man*, Hughes decided to retire from writing novels. Her family obligations had become too great. She was caring for a sick mother and her grandchildren. She couldn't find the time or the peace needed to write her textured novels. However, she did continue to review mysteries and read extensively in the genre while attending to her domestic problems. She kept her finger on the pulse of mysteries by her frequent reviews and she served on the Best Novel committee for the Edgars for several years running.

Over the years, a number of feminists have railed against Hughes for giving up a highly successful career to tend to the home. She was not sympathetic to their point-of-view. She was happy with her life and family. Most of the work of raising the children fell to Hughes, who said that her husband held rather old-fashioned views where child-rearing belonging to the wife. Carrying the bulk of the responsibility, Hughes didn't complain about the work. She was assisted by members of her family and paid help who took care of things around the house while she wrote. She felt happy with the level of support she received. Even with help, Hughes abandoned writing for more than a decade.

After nearly a fifteen-year hiatus, Hughes bounded back on the mystery scene. In 1978, she was awarded the MWA Grand Master award for her contributions to the genre. "I never thought of myself in terms of the Grand Master. I was too young to be Grand Master at that time; that was for old folks."[10]

The honor came the same year that her biography of Erle Stanley Gardner was published. Hughes had known Gardner and wrote *Erle Stanley Gardner: The Case of the Real Perry Mason* following his death to commemorate his life and contributions to mystery. At the time, not many mystery authors had been studied or written about. In her words, she credited her assignment to her critical work in the genre. "I don't know why I was chosen, but I believe that in a circui-

---

10. Oral History Interview with Dorothy B. Hughes. Center for Southwest Research, General Library, University of New Mexico.

tous way credit can be traced to Digby Diehl, my book editor at the *Los Angeles Times*, where I have been mystery critic for more than ten years. Digby had the perception to recognize the stature of Gardner, and probably, not surprisingly, the wish to single him out for special tribute. At any rate, I was asked to write 'A' reviews on the Gardner books that came out in Gardner's later years. The 'A' is the long review at the *Times* and this enabled me to consider the importance of Gardner's work as a whole, not piece by piece. I don't know, but it is entirely possible that it was from reading some of these reviews that Mr. Hughes [the president of William Morrow and Company] selected me."[11]

Hughes' book was one of the few books written at the time that critically looks at the man's life and his writing and how the two related. Gardner wrote at a phenomenal pace and lived his life in the same manner. He was a force to be reckoned with in everything he touched and Hughes captured his indominatable spirit in her biography of him.

The biography of the writer would be the final book produced by Hughes. She retired from writing mystery reviews the following year and returned to her family life. She died on May 6, 1993.

---

11. Hughes, Dorothy B. *Erle Stanley Gardner: The Case of the Real Perry Mason*, William Morrow and Company (New York, 1978), page 6-7.

Similar Authors Published Today:

- Dean James
- Lev Raphael
- Daniel Stashower
- Max Allen Collins

Bibliography

Dark Certainty - - - - - - - - - - - - - -1931
(*poems*)
**Pueblo On The Mesa: The First Fifty Years Of The Uni-
versity Of New Mexico** - - - - - - - - - - -1939
The Cross-Eyed Bear- - - - - - - - - - - -1940
The So Blue Marble - - - - - - - - - - - -1940
The Bamboo Blonde - - - - - - - - - - - -1941
The Fallen Sparrow - - - - - - - - - - - -1942
(*Film: 1943, directed by Richard Wallace, starring John
Garfield*)
The Blackbirder - - - - - - - - - - - - - -1943
The Delicate Ape - - - - - - - - - - - - - -1944
Johnnie- - - - - - - - - - - - - - - - - -1944
Dread Journey - - - - - - - - - - - - - - -1945
Ride The Pink Horse - - - - - - - - - - - -1946
(*Film: 1947, directed by Robert Montgomery, screenplay by
Ben Hecht and Charles Lederer. - Remade in 1964 for TV as*
The Hanged Man, *directed by Don Siegel.*)
The Scarlet Imperial / Kiss For A Killer - - 1946
In A Lonely Place - - - - - - - - - - - - -1947
(*Film: 1950, directed by Nicholas Ray, starring Humphrey
Bogart and Gloria Grahame.*)
The Big Barbecue - - - - - - - - - - - - -1949
The Candy Kid- - - - - - - - - - - - - - -1950
The Davidian Report- - - - - - - - - - - 1952
(*alternate title: The Body On The Bench*)
The Expendable Man- - - - - - - - - - - -1963
**Erle Stanley Gardner: The Case Of The Real Perry
Mason**- - - - - - - - - - - - - - - - - -1978

CHAPTER 5 — Charlotte Armstrong

If one author epitomized 1950s popular culture, it was Charlotte Armstrong. From Marilyn Monroe to Alfred Hitchcock, Vera Miles and other stars of the time, Armstrong, through her strong body of mysteries, touched them all.

Her work covered a multitude of places and themes, but Armstrong had a particular fondness for thrillers set in the family. Even though most of her work is out of print today, one of her post-war novels, *The Chocolate Cobweb*, was awarded a Prix Louis Delluc in 2001 for its screen interpretation.

Charlotte Armstrong was born May 2, 1905 in Vulcan, Michigan, a small mining town on the upper peninsula of the state. Her father was the chief engineer for the mining company as well as the inventor of a number of safety mechanisms for easier and better blasting equipment.

Charl, as her family called her, was strongly influenced by her father. She recalls wanting to write from a very early age. "I wanted to write about as soon as I could read. Earned my very first 5¢ when, aged 11, I wrote a play, cast it, directed it, produced it in a neighbors [sic] barn."[1]

Armstrong switched from a public school in Vulcan to an all-girl's school, Ferry Hall, outside of Chicago. After graduation, she attended the University of Wisconsin for two years and transferred to Barnard College at Columbia University where she received her B.A. in 1925. She would later state that she switched schools to get an introduction to New York City.

She enjoyed New York so much that she decided to get a job to remain there. "After being graduated I wasn't going back to the middle west, not me, so I got a job taking classified ads on the phone for *The New York Times*. I was the guinea pig in the testing of the use of typewriters in this department. That's why they hired a college graduate."[2] While at the *Times*, Armstrong met Jack Lewi, whom she later married. Armstrong was a fashion design reporter by then, working for *Breath of the Avenue*, "up and down Fifth Avenue going into lots of department stores as a spy." She was later fired from *Breath of the Avenue* and went to work for a firm of accountants. That job left her plenty of free time in the office, which Armstrong used to write poetry. She was encouraged by her efforts when *The New Yorker* published a few of her early works.

After the birth of the Lewi's first son in 1928, the couple lived in Manhattan, then Boomfield, New Jersey, and later moved in with Jack's brother in Glen Ridge during the Depression. Armstrong began writing stage plays to help make ends meet. Her first play was produced in Cape Cod, but never made it to Broadway. She often compared her time in the theater as service like Jacob's long wait to marry Rachel. The time paid off as her next effort was a tragedy entitled *The Happiest Days*, which was produced on Broadway in 1938 where it lasted only a few days.

She didn't give up after this effort, though she changed the tone of her next play. *Ring Around Elizabeth* was a comedy that opened on Broadway after rave reviews in Philadelphia. Produced by

1. Press Release from Coward-McCann, April 2, 1959, quote from Charlotte Armstrong.
2. Press Release from Coward-McCann, April 2, 1959, quote from Charlotte Armstrong.

Alfred Bloomingdale, the play only lasted a week on Broadway before closing.

While battling the flu, Armstrong read a series of mysteries and decided to write one of her own. She found writing novels easier to manage with married life. She didn't need to spend hours locked away in hotel rooms, rewriting a script based on the whims of the producer, director, or angel of the production. She wrote most every morning on typewriter or long-hand. Even so, she found that the earlier stage training let her write her books in terms of scenes and dialogue.

Armstrong started her career writing the same sort of detective novel as many of the other Golden Age writers. Her detective, Mac-Dougal Duff, is a former history teacher who has retired from education to solve mysteries. His method is a mixture of common sense and detection. He tracks the history of the characters to find the solution. He follows the alibis and timetables to eliminate people from suspicion, leaving a solitary person as the guilty party.

MacDuff was a character from Macbeth and Duff expresses his disdain for people who invariably quote and misquote the "Lay On, MacDuff" line from the play. Armstrong was a fan of Shakespeare and veiled references to many of his plays find their way into her books. Armstrong admits to being a fan. A newspaper interview told, "She borrowed books from the neighbors and read the complete works of Shakespeare when she was still too young to understand the meaning of all the words, but loved their sounds."[3]

In *Lay On, Mac Duff*, the narrator, Bessie Gibbon, comes to New York City to try her luck in town after her parents pass away. She is taken into the home of her wealthy uncle who spoils her with material possessions. She quickly becomes enmeshed in a murder mystery when her uncle's business partner is found murdered at home. The four businessmen had been playing a ruthless game of Parcheesi in which her uncle lost. This rare occurrence caused her uncle, Charles Cathcart, to throw his specially made Parcheesi pieces out of the win-

---

3. "Author's Second Novel, Play to Become Films", *Glendale News-Press*, August 2, 1948.

dows. When one of the pieces appears on one of his Parcheesi competitors' corpse, suspicion falls on Cathcart.

Another one of the foursome falls victim to the killer and Bessie tries to get to the bottom of the mysterious happenings in order to clear her uncle, to whom she feels a debt of gratitude. Despite her relationship to the narrator, Charles Cathcart is not portrayed in a positive light. Although he is definitely Bessie's benefactor, he can be ruthless and manipulative in her presence. He won his much younger wife as part of a business deal. By book's end, it appears that the Cathcarts have a true loving relationship, but the genesis of the relationship is still suspect. Additionally, he plays Parcheesi more competitively then many people pursue Olympic sports. The hard edge of his personality is not hidden from the reader. The book has an odd feel to it since the main suspect is someone that the reader can easily be ambivalent about.

The book is a fairly straightforward whodunit with roots in Cathcart's business past and a cast of interesting characters. J.J. Jones, a good-looking reporter who falls hard for Bessie, introduces Mac Duff to the case. Duff is described by Bessie as "All Duff's long limbs balanced themselves quietly as he stood there. His color was quiet, from the clothes he wore to the quiet brown of his inconspicuous neat hair. His eyes were hazel, I guess, neither blue nor brown, and the lids over them were heavy and fallen at the corners as if they were tired of keeping open to watch what he understood too well.

He had a melancholy face, seamed and lined as if he had been through a lot, and yet the lines were lightly etched as if for a long time some peacefulness of spirit had been working to erase them. I couldn't tell how old he was, but like my uncle he knew too much to be young."[4] Duff quickly comes across the solution to the case. In true first Golden Age fashion, he calls all the main suspects together in order to reveal a killer. The solution, while not patently obvious, is apparent to a discerning reader with an eye to the possible romances in the book.

4. Charlotte Armstrong, *Lay On, Mac Duff* (New York: Coward-McCann, 1942), page 83.

Mac Duff only appeared in the first three of Armstrong's works. She would quickly realize that her true talent rested in the suspense field. In her second book, *The Case of the Weird Sisters*, Mac Duff is called to the scene of an attempted murder of a rich industrialist with three older disabled half-sisters. The odd scenario is reminiscent of some of Ellery Queen's early works, especially books like *There Was an Old Woman*. One sister is blind, another deaf, and the third has only the use of one arm. These three sisters, much like the witches of Macbeth, put a curse on Innes Whitlock, their half-brother.

Innes, along with his young fiancee Alice, is forced to stay in the house with the sisters after their car breaks down. While visiting with his sisters, Innes takes stock of their situation and mandates changes in their living arrangements. Innes falls ill after dinner, when he eats some veal that causes him to have an allergic reaction, a condition known to his sisters. After dinner, accidents begin to happen with all of them pointing to one or all of the sisters as the prime suspects. Alice is a former student of Mac Duff and calls on him for help, after she sees him at the local train station.

The book's main flaw is the lack of truly sympathetic characters in the book. Each of the three sisters is portrayed in unflattering terms, with the deaf sister, who is also fat and slovenly, coming off the worst. Innes is whiny and uncertain. Alice admits to only marrying Innes for his money and is up front about her mercenary motives. With so few characters to care about, the book is not one of her best works.

Armstrong rounded out this trilogy with *Innocent Flower*. Her books left the detective field after this last excursion with Mac Duff. Armstrong gave up her character after this and began to write stand-alone books. While many mystery authors found that the suspense field could be lucrative, several detective fiction authors, like Ellery Queen and Erle Stanley Gardner, found success while still using the same main character.

Armstrong changed her genre with her next work, *The Unsuspected*. Her agent, Bernice Baumgartner of Brandt and Brandt, encouraged the author to write in the suspense field. Her work immediately started to receive more recognition after changing genres. *The Unsuspected* was serialized in *The Saturday Evening Post* in 1945, and Warner Brothers later produced a film version of the book with Claude Rains. As in so many cases, her fame grew exponentially when her works became vehicles for the big screen.

The book was also instrumental in the lives of the Lewis. The Lewis moved west to California where the family settled in Glendale. The family had relatives in the area and would live there for the next 25 years. They made their home at 1700 Grandview Avenue, across the street from Casey Stengel, the famed baseball manager. Additionally, Armstrong's son Jack left home about the same time to go to MIT in Boston.

With fewer money worries and nearly grown children, Armstrong found interesting ways to study character for her writing. She would later say that "a woman with a family has an excellent opportunity to study character, which she considers the first and most important step to writing. Constant observation of people, places and situations, in her opinion, should become a habit if one wishes to write."[5] True to her word, most of Armstrong's work focuses on the family and the terror that can happen within the realms of the home.

With the success of *The Unsuspected*, Armstrong turned her back on the whodunit field and plunged headlong into suspense, where she excelled. "I find I killed off fewer and fewer characters all the time," she said in later interviews.

True to her word, her next novel, *The Chocolate Cobweb*, had no murder in the course of the book and the murderer was revealed in the first chapter. Instead, the book is a study in the cold plotting of revenge and a thriller with almost no violence, few conventional suspense sequences, and a serene family surface that covers a multitude of hidden motives and agendas.

The book begins with the offhanded comment by a cousin to Amanda Garth, revealing to her that the hospital had made a mix-up at the time of Amanda's birth. Amanda is immediately drawn to the other baby's father, Tobias Garrison, since she recently lost her own father.

5. "Personalities in the Scene", *Glendale Independent*, February 16, 1964.

The connection is convincing, because Amanda has elected to study art and Tobias is a well-respected artist.

His most famous painting, "Belle in the Doorway", takes Amanda's breath away when she sees the work at an exhibition of his art. The romantic air of the painting makes her want to meet this man.

Her initial introduction to the family is met with suspicion. At the instigation of instantly hospitable Ione, who is both first and third wife to Tobias, Amanda stays for supper. After being embarrassed by the family, Amanda mimics a trait of Belle's that was shared with her by a family friend. The mood of the household changes immediately. After her charade, Amanda observes, unseen, Ione deliberately spilling a thermos of chocolate she's prepared for Thone, the true son of Tobias and Belle. The action exposes the contradictions of this perilously balanced household – the disheveled quasi-addict-artist-husband, his rich, possessive wife, and Belle's sullen son. The nightcap, Amanda learns after a lab analysis by Gene, her sometimes beau, was laced with a sleeping drug. Ione opted not to poison Thone after she becomes uncertain as to whether or not the boy is really Belle's child – or if Amanda could possibly be the true child of Tobias and Belle.

From there, the book turns into a battle of wits and wills between the pragmatic Amanda who places herself in harm's way to be around the genius who might be her father and the handsome Thone, whom she has met, and her smiling, friendly, ever-gracious hostess, who may be a murderess.

While the book makes no pretense of who is the murderer and why the crimes were committed, the means of the acts are not revealed until the final pages. This uncertainty makes the characters move with hesitation in their desire to bring Ione to justice and keeps the reader guessing as to how and when the end might come for Amanda and perhaps Thone as well.

Armstrong's work only grew stronger with her next book. Her bestseller *Mischief* became the basis for the movie *Don't Bother to Knock*, which starred a young Marilyn Monroe as a mentally unbalanced baby-sitter. As in *Bus Stop*, Monroe gives some of her best work, proof that she was more than just a dumb blonde. *Mischief* would do for babysitters what *Psycho* would later do for showers. Armstrong's book started out as a play entitled *Little Nell*, a wry twist on the idea of the poor young Dickensian heroine. She later changed the story to the now familiar plot of the babysitter who seems reliable, but quickly displays her disturbed nature. The elevator man's niece is a last minute replacement for the husband's sister who had a previous engagement. Nell, the babysitter, seems almost mentally challenged at first, but her total lack of morals and concern for the future are slowly revealed to the reader. The book is tightly and expertly written and touches upon the fears of every parent.

Two themes begin to resonate through the works of Armstrong at this point. The first is the idea of the strong woman. Women who might appear slight in appearance, but are made of steel inside have replaced the dependent girls of her first few efforts. In *Mischief*, Ruth Jones, the child's mother, is one such heroine. For three quarters of the book, she is merely the companion to her husband who has just wowed an audience with his speech. She is only given a few polite words to murmur in appreciation of her spouse. However, when she feels concern about her daughter being in danger, she immediately rushes to action. She travels through New York City alone and confronts Nell without thought to her own safety. "Ruth had not always been a gracious young matron, a pretty wife, a gentle mother. In her day she'd climbed many a tough tree and hung by knobby knees off ladders with pigtails dragging. And she'd chased the other kids off rafts and over rooftops... She'd had her bruises and given them. The world of direct physical conflict, violent and painful, had not always been beyond her ken... There was lightening on her eyeballs as she got her hands in that yellowish hair and yanked and the girl screeched and fell forward, twisting, and Ruth rolled on the hard floor to get from under her."[6] These women are typically married, happy, and most strong in defending a family member.

The other idea that starts to come through in her work is the

---

6. Charlotte Armstrong, *Mischief, A Charlotte Armstrong Treasury* (New York: Coward McCann, 1972), page 286.

idea of a collective unconscious. Armstrong would use the notion in many of her later novels. The subtle idea that a number of characters could share an emotion without discussing it appears in a number of her works. In *Mischief*, she manages to imbue several of her characters with the realization that they share the guilt for this situation. The child's brush with danger from the deranged babysitter could have been prevented with intervention from any number of people. All the characters "could" have done something to stop the crescendo of fear and abuse. While none of the characters express this concern verbally, it passes through the thoughts of several of the major characters. The couple staying downstairs might have investigated the crying earlier or the elevator operator might have suggested another babysitter. Thematically tied to the idea of helping each other, Jed, Nell's date for the evening, even recalls a fight he had with another woman about her desire to give money to the bums on the streets. The notion of contributing to help others runs deep in the novel.

She followed this book by *The Dream Walker*, a tense psychological thriller about a scheme to ruin a man through innuendo. The book reveals the plot to discredit John Paul Marcus in the first few pages of the story. Marcus had discovered another man's treason and reported it. As the traitor languishes in jail, he determines that Marcus is responsible for all of his troubles and vows revenge. He hires a wonder boy to help devise the scheme and puts the plan into motion.

The actual plot of the book is one of Armstrong's weaker efforts. She gives the bare bones of the plot in the first few pages. The novel only needs Armstrong to fill in the details. While it is fascinating to watch the genius at work while Marcum is framed for treason, the story holds minimal suspense at the build-up to the event.

The book is a strong study of the detriments of gossip and speculation. While the first few events of the book are well-documented by investigators and reporters, as the seemingly paranormal phenomenon of astral projection continue, the press becomes lax. That allows the conspirators to frame Marcus with the smear of speculation about his activities without evidence. The reader, especially looking at the book in hindsight, gets the impression that Armstrong was making a statement about McCarthyism and the Communist witch hunts that plagued the film industry in Southern California at that time.

In 1956, she would publish her defining book, *A Dram of Poison*, which would win the best novel Edgar for 1956. Despite its label as a crime novel, the book has no murder, no villain and no crimes. At times, Armstrong chafed at the label of mystery novelist and even suspense writer.

A Dram of Poison opens quietly, with the introduction of Kenneth Gibson, the middle-aged man who makes the unlikely hero of the book. He marries the daughter of a fellow professor at his school after the man's death in order to save her from a life of poverty and despair. As he coaxes his new bride back to life, he discovers that he is falling in love with her. However, a car wreck occurs before he can share his feelings.

The arrival of his sister, Ethel, to assist with his recovery provides the impetus for most of the action. Ethel's jaded attitude is tinged with pseudo-Freudian advice. To her, the auto accident was a subliminal message from his wife that she wanted to dispose of him and find a new younger lover. The man next door happens to fit the bill perfectly. To her brother and patient, she hammers home the fact that he is a father figure to his young wife, not a mate, and that he should not have been so foolish in his choices.

The constant pressure continues until Gibson steals poison to do away with himself. Instead, he forgets the poison, which is stored in an olive oil bottle, and leaves it on a crowded city bus. The rest of the novel takes a growing group of people who get involved with Gibson and his wife as they struggle to find the poison before someone uses it in the preparation of their evening meal.

The quest to find the poison becomes an accumulation of characters as the Gibsons locate the bus driver who finds a blonde girl from the bus who remembers a socialite who recalls an artist on the same bus. The hodge-podge of characters becomes an impromptu celebration of the uncertainty of life. The characters don't agree on all topics, but the message is one of hope and redemption, not a life built on subconscious desires and actions.

"You extrapolate a future on what's known now. You extend the old lines. What you don't take into account are the surprises.

"'Hey! said the bus driver. 'Hey! Hey!'

"'Every big jump is a surprise, a revelation,' lectured the artist, 'and a tangent off the old. Penicillin. Atom splitting. Who guessed they were coming?'

"'Exactly,' cried Virginia. 'Or the wheel? Or television? How do we know what's coming next?' She was all excited. 'Maybe some whole vast opening up in a direction we've hardly even though of...'"[7]

Unlike most mystery novels, the book contains no murder and no violence. The novel is a tribute to how random, wonderful, and surprising life can be. Indeed, by the end of the book, the problems have been solved and the issue of Ethel has been satisfactorily dealt with.

While the mystery genre claimed her as their own, Armstrong defined her work as unique, but familiar to readers. "I am looking for an idea that is new and startling and yet, humanly speaking, old and familiar. Also it should be dramatic but real... quick but deep. and it must wind up in a solution that is unexpected and yet clonks down on the reader as the only possible true outcome."[8]

Even with her burgeoning fame as a writer of fiction, Armstrong was still enamored of the stage. Being so close to Hollywood and having seen some of her novels recreated on the screen, she decided to write for television. One of her early assignments was with the master of suspense, Alfred Hitchcock, as he created his famous television show. Prior to *The Alfred Hitchcock Hour*, Hitchcock directed three other shows for television. One of those shows, "Ford Startime," first aired on April 5, 1960. An episode titled "Incident At A Corner"

---

7. Charlotte Armstrong, *A Dram of Poison*, (New York: Coward McCann, 1956), page 134.
8. Letter to Anthony Boucher, White mss., Manuscripts Department, Lilly Library, Indiana University, Bloomington, Indiana, dated April 9, 1960.

(written by Armstrong) was based on one of her own short stories. Stars in that episode included Vera Miles, Paul Hartman and George Peppard.

With amazing versatility, Armstrong not only wrote stage plays, teleplays, and novels, she penned a number of well-written short stories as well. Her shorter works appeared under pseudonyms. Her works have been published, reprinted and anthologized over the years. Using the Mike Russell pseudonym, she published a short story titled "The Enemy" in the May 1951 issue of *Ellery Queen's Mystery Magazine* later reprinted in the June 1991 issue. A fantasy novelette she wrote titled "Three Day Magic" was published 4 times: first in a 1948 issue of the *Magazine of Fantasy & Science Fiction*, then reprinted in the same magazine in September 1952 (at a time when Anthony Boucher was an editor of the magazine), and then printed in two 1986 anthologies titled *Strange Maine* and *Isaac Asimov's Magical Worlds of Fantasy #7: Magical Wishes*.

Armstrong also wrote under the pseudonym Jo Valentine. Despite the fact that her novels that had little relation to crime fiction, her mainstream fiction appeared under a pen name. "Older and perhaps wiser now. I squirm at the confines of the 'suspense' story. So I have for a long time written short stories that are not suspense. And sold them too. Hauled off and wrote a novel some years ago. Set in the mining town of my own childhood. And it was put out under the name of Jo Valentine. It didn't do too badly a for a first novel by an unknown."[9]

Armstrong's prodigious output seemed to increase as she grew older. In 1963, she released five new books. One of those novels, *The Witch's House*, was a suspense novel with no murder and little gore. Two professors disappear from a local school one evening. The readers are told exactly what has happened to them, but the characters in the book are left to determine what went wrong. The few clues that are left for them are not sufficient to find the missing men immediately.

Again Armstrong provides a strong woman character in Anabel O'Shea, the wife of one of the missing professors. She immediate-

9. Press Release from Coward-McCann, April 2, 1959, quote from Charlotte Armstrong.

ly is disenchanted with the response from the university and the police, who believe that her husband, Pat, might have run off with another woman or skipped out on his responsibilities. She is not comforted by their effort, "some marvelous cure-all, called an APB."

The titular witch is also drawn as a strong woman, albeit one who has lost touch with society and reality. Mrs. Pryde, the woman who takes in Pat O'Shea, is portrayed effectively as a witch. Harkening back to her depiction of the three sisters in *The Case of the Weird Sisters*, this woman mutters about lost children and lives in her own world, where her son is still alive and has come home to be with his family. The fear of her differences makes the neighbors shy away from interacting with Mrs. Pryde, and further fosters the witch image that she has.

Armstrong paints a rather bleak picture of the educational system in America. The school is more interested in maintaining a low profile and battling rumors of defections to Communist countries rather than finding the two men. The "authorities" are very more concerned in maintaining the status quo, and it falls to Anabel and the daughter of the other missing professor to find the men. The two women, who have been marginalized by the police and school, are the ones who actually see that justice is done in the society. The one child who notices the missing man on his way to the witch's house is physically challenged and has the time to watch for the cars. However, no one else in the neighborhood believes his story of a man who went down the road and never came back.

Even with her prodigious output of these years, the quality of her work remained exceptional. At 62, she wrote not one but two of the year's Edgar nominations for best novel of the year. *The Gift Shop* and *Lemon in the Basket* were both nominated, but lost to Donald Westlake's *God Save the Mark*. The books highlight a trend in Armstrong's writings. While she had written domestic masterpieces like *The Chocolate Cobweb* in the past, all of Armstrong's later books focus on the family milieu.

In *The Gift Shop*, the story deals with the long-lost daughter of a wealthy and powerful man. The man has three sons, but longs for a little girl, who might be out there somewhere. His existing progeny include the governor of a state and a prominent surgeon. The third son, Harry Fairchild, is something of a slacker. Fairchild receives a phone call from his friend, a private detective. Before dying of stab wounds at the airport, the detective leaves a cryptic message with Fairchild. The private eye has taken great precautions to hide the little girl from people who want to influence the governor — so great that no one can find the girl. Fairchild hires the young woman who works in the airport gift shop to accompany him on a worldwide search for the little girl. While the search and the implications of the villains take on a global sphere, the heart of the novel and the motivation come from the domestic front. In the end, the villains of the book are motivated from a warped sense of family.

Children are featured prominently in this book, where the major clue is a piggy bank. Children always seem to come in threes in an Armstrong book, reflecting her own family—two boys and a girl. While the families are located around the globe, each family is shown to be its own special entity. The families range from parents on vacation with their spoiled youngster to a girl who is virtually held prisoner by her overprotective nanny.

Even with the concentration on family, Armstrong uses a charming insight. In this scene, Armstrong gives her opinion about the pecking order in children. "[T]he bigger ones must watch out for the little ones, and the boys must watch out for the girls and the girls must watch out for everybody, of course."[10] Such humorous insights into family dynamics make the book even tenser by juxtaposing the comical with the terror of an outside influence touching the family. Armstrong takes the domestic scenario and puts the characters in danger. As with *Mischief*'s babysitter, the real terror lies within the realm of everyday life, not in the world outside.

Her other Edgar nominee that year, *Lemon in the Basket*, is a phrase used by one of the characters in this novel as a means of de-

10. Charlotte Armstrong, *The Gift Shop*, *The Charlotte Armstrong Festival* (New York: Coward McCann, 1975), page 195.

scribing her husband, a less-than-average man in a family of stellar performers. Rufus has gone through any number of get-rich-quick vocations, compared to his brothers who are a college professor and a well-known surgeon. His wife married Rufus for the chance to improve her social standing, although nothing of the sort seems to happen with a man who fails at every profession he tries.

The book opens with each family member making an announcement about his or her most recent achievement. "The talk must turn. It was right and proper for the family to toast those of its members who had been honored by the world. Six out of eight! And to enjoy all this in concert. It was right and proper to celebrate each individual's achievement, but the Tylers were not going into a long session of group-gloating. Not if Maggie could help it, and she could. Tamsen approved."[11]

The action begins when the young grandson of a Middle Eastern ruler comes to the U. S. for surgery performed by the surgeon in the Tyler family. The royal family are friends of the Tylers and stay with the family during the ordeal. The stakes for correcting the grandson's medical condition are raised as the Middle Eastern country begins to spout anti-American rhetoric and rounds up a number of American professors in the country as dissidents and spies. While the Tylers try to keep the surgery quiet for international reasons, Rufus notifies the press and begins a subtle plan of sabotage against his family. His jealousy and feelings of inadequacy are played out against the politics of the Middle East.

In 1968, Armstrong donated the majority of her papers and manuscripts to the Special Collections at Boston University. She had learned that she had cancer and wanted to give copies of her work to the university. She left most of correspondence as well as stories and novel manuscripts.

In the same year, she completed *The Balloon Man*. The story revolves around Sherry Reynard, the wife of a struggling writer, who

---

11. Charlotte Armstrong, *Lemon in the Basket*, *The Charlotte Armstrong Festival* (New York: Coward McCann, 1975), page 222.

is beaten by her husband, Ward, while he is experimenting with LSD. The acid trip causes him to lash out at his wife and child, causing their son to go to the hospital. Sherry leaves her husband and takes up residence in a small boarding house near the hospital that is due to be demolished soon. The boarding house is filled with quirky characters who support Sherry and her child in her quest for freedom.

Sherry's in-laws denounce her as an unfit parent, and vow to take her son by any means necessary. They cut her off without any money to support herself or her son. In the meantime, they coddle their son, making excuses for his behavior under the influence of hallucinogens. The young man is no condition to be a husband or father as he struggles with the drugs. In order to secure their grandson, the Reynards offer to return the family firm to Cliff Storm, a friend of Ward's, if the young man will spy on Sherry. They blame Sherry for taking their son down the wrong path into drugs and an early marriage that tied him down with children. Her early dance career is referred to as being a showgirl, stripper or cocktail waitress.

Storm pretends to run into her at the hospital and finds out where Sherry lives. He moves into the same boarding house as Sherry. She begins to doubt her own sanity as Storm begins to spy on her and gather evidence for a custody hearing. Again the drama is a family one as two sets of parents do what they deem best to secure the future of their children.

Armstrong completed her final book just before her death on July 19, 1969, the same day that man walked on the moon for the first time. A professional to the end, Armstrong finished *The Protégé* during her final days in the hospital. The book was published posthumously.

Even after death, praise and accolades continued. Claude Chabrol, longtime master of the French domestic thriller, filmed "Merci pour la Chocolat" in 1999, based on *The Chocolate Cobweb*. The film was considered a masterpiece. The movie earned Chabrol the 2000 Prix Louis Delluc, an even more prestigious film prize than the French Oscar ("Cesar"). Set mostly in a manor home in Switzerland, the story was changed to reflect the French influence on the plot: Isabelle Huppert stars as Marie-Claire Muller-Polonski, or "Mika," who owns and operates a Swiss chocolate factory. She re-marries a concert pianist (instead of an artist), Andre Polonski played by Jacques Dutronc. In the film, Mika is wealthy from her family's gourmet chocolate—which she may have used to kill her husband's other wife.

Charlotte Armstrong's family made news again with a real-life murder mystery that occurred a few years after her death. Her husband, Jack Lewi, surprised a burglar upon returning to his home and was killed by the intruder. Three days later, Stephen Jackson was arrested for the murder. He was the Lewi's gardener at the time of the murder. He later pled guilty to second-degree murder and was sent to jail.

Similar Authors Published Today:

- Frances Fyfield
- Minette Walters
- Mary Willis Walker
- Laurie R. King
- Ruth Rendell
- Sharyn McCrumb

Bibliography

Lay On, Mac Duff! - - - - - - - - - - - - - 1942
The Case of the Weird Sisters - - - - - - - 1943
(Film: The Three Weird Sisters, 1948, directed by Daniel Birt)
The Innocent Flower - - - - - - - - - - - - 1945
(UK Title: Death Filled the Glass)
The Unsuspected - - - - - - - - - - - - - - 1946
(Film: The Unsuspected, 1947, directed by Michael Curtiz,
  starring Claude Rains)
The Chocolate Cobweb - - - - - - - - - - - 1948
(Film: Merci pour le chocolat, 2000, directed by Claude
  Chabrol)
Mischief - - - - - - - - - - - - - - - - - - 1950
(Film: Don't Bother to Knock, 1952, directed by Roy Ward
  Baker, starring Marilyn Monroe)
The Black-Eyed Stranger - - - - - - - - - - 1951
Catch-As-Catch-Can - - - - - - - - - - - 1952
(Also published as: Walk Out on Death)
The Better to Eat You - - - - - - - - - - - 1954
(Also published as: Murder's Nest)
The Dream Walker - - - - - - - - - - - - 1955
(Also published as: Alibi for Murder)
A Dram of Poison - - - - - - - - - - - - - 1956
(Edgar Award)
The Albatross - - - - - - - - - - - - - - - 1957
(shorts stories)
Duo - 1959
(2 novelets)
The Seventeen Widows of San Souci - - - - 1959
Something Blue - - - - - - - - - - - - - - 1962
Then Came Two Women - - - - - - - - - - 1962
A Little Less Than Kind - - - - - - - - - - 1963
The Mark of the Hand - - - - - - - - - - - 1963
The One-Faced Girl - - - - - - - - - - - - 1963
Who's Been Sitting in My Chair? - - - - - - 1963

The Witch's House - - - - - - - - - - - 1963
The Turret Room - - - - - - - - - - - - 1965
Dream of Fair Woman - - - - - - - - - - 1966

I See You - - - - - - - - - - - - - - - - 1966
(short stories)
The Gift Shop - - - - - - - - - - - - - - 1967
Lemon in the Basket - - - - - - - - - - - 1967
The Balloon Man - - - - - - - - - - - - 1968
(Film: La Rupture, 1970, directed by Claude Chabrol)
Seven Seats to the Moon - - - - - - - - - 1969
The Protégé - - - - - - - - - - - - - - - 1970

As Jo Valentine
The Trouble in Thor - - - - - - - - - - - 1953
(Also published as: And Sometimes Death)

CHAPTER 6 — Patricia Highsmith

Few authors start at the top of their form, but Patricia Highsmith claimed this honor with the release of her first novel, *Strangers on a Train*, later produced as an Alfred Hitchcock film. That feat alone made her a household name, but she had much more to come. She also created one of the most infamous characters in mystery fiction, Tom Ripley, the materialistic, amoral protagonist who has appeared in four films to date. Over the span of her 40 year career, Highsmith would go on to win the O. Henry Memorial Award, MWA's Edgar award, *Le Grand Prix de Litterature Policiere*, and the Award of the Crime Writers' Association of Great Britain.

Patricia Plangman was born in Fort Worth, Texas, on January 19, 1921, to commercial artist parents. Before she was even born, her parents separated. While her mother legally retained custody of the baby, Highsmith's maternal grandmother reared Patricia for several years. Highsmith would later recall that time period as the happiest of her life.

When Highsmith was three years old, her mother remarried. Patricia's new surname came from Stanley Highsmith, her stepfather.

At age six, Highsmith and her family moved from Texas to New York. Highsmith was given every indication that her stepfather was indeed her birthfather although he did not formally adopt her for several years. Highsmith was 12 before she learned the truth about her parentage and met her birthfather.

Not only was Highsmith confused about her parentage, her relationship with her mother was acrimonious. She later told stories about her mother, saying that the woman routinely taunted her with how she had tried to abort Highsmith during her pregnancy. Highsmith's mother would say that her daughter's affection for painting came from an attempted abortion from swallowing turpentine.

The repeated traumas with her parents and the frequent moves left Highsmith as a loner. Throughout her life, Highsmith had dalliances, but never formed a long-term union. She spent most of her life alone. Even friends kept their distance. "Her sometime publisher Otto Penzler described her as a 'mean, cruel, hard, unlovable, unloving human being.'" [1], in one recorded interview. A former lover remembers Highsmith as angry, and anti-everybody.

Similarly, Highsmith held a dim view of the humans around her. Rarely did Highsmith say anything positive about family in her writings. The dysfunction and the lies in her own life came through in her work, though she denied that her past was fodder for her novels. Even in the details, her difficulties with her family was apparent. Many of her ill-fated protagonists are commercial artists, the profession of her parents.

After moving to New York City with her mother and stepfather, she attended Julia Richmond High School. She later studied at Barnard College at Columbia University where she edited the literary magazine and graduated with a B.A. in 1942. While she'd shown artistic talent at an early age, Highsmith dabbled in many creative

1. The Guardian Unlimited, London, England, January 28, 2000

pursuits before settling on writing. She was a talented sculptress and painter as well as writer.

Her earliest writings, at the age of 15, show signs of her later fiction, dealing with strange characters and criminal activities. While few if any of Highsmith's books could be considered mystery novels, most of her work is categorized as suspense. The stories contain a crime and tension as to whether or not the perpetrators will be brought to justice. Highsmith would later write that she resented the suspense categorization in the United States, because she felt that the label limited her reviews and her sales. Indeed, her popularity in the U.S. never rivaled her recognition in Europe.

As she continued to write short stories during her twenties, Highsmith managed to support herself with a number of jobs. At one point, she worked in a department store, a job that played a role in her later work. She wrote for comic books as well. In 1945, her first short story, *The Heroine*, was published in *Harper's Bazaar*. The story had not come out in her school's literary magazine because it was deemed "unsuitable" for the school.

On a recommendation from Truman Capote (whose work she admired), she went to stay at the Yaddo writers' colony in Sarasota Springs, New York in the late 1940s. The time of quiet and reflection suited Highsmith well. She never forgot her debt to the writers' colony; she included a bequest to it in her will. While staying at Yaddo, Highsmith redrafted her novel, *Strangers on a Train*, and soon after found a publisher, Harper & Sons. While *Strangers on a Train* would be her first published novel, Highsmith had two other unpublished manuscripts sitting in a drawer by the time she went to Yaddo.

Her first novel was a sensation. The story follows the exploits of two men who meet on a train, Guy Haines and Charles Anthony Bruno. Bruno thinks that he recognizes a sympathetic friend in Guy. Both men having unpleasant family members who stand in the way of their perceived happiness. Even though she is pregnant with another man's baby, Guy's wife Miriam refuses to divorce him so he can marry another woman. Bruno's father has tight control over the family purse strings and won't let Bruno have enough money to live the life he wants. Both have reasons to want someone dead, but the respective murders would point to Haines and Bruno as the guilty parties. Bruno suggests that they swap murders, so that no suspicion is thrown on to the person with the motive. Without motive, the killings became random violence, rather than premeditated murder.

While Guy shrugs off the idea as the talk of a crazy stranger, Bruno takes the conversation seriously and kills Guy's estranged wife, Miriam. Bruno insinuates himself into Guy's life until Guy is forced to kill Bruno's father. The detective Gerard uses the resulting guilt and shame to trap the two characters.

In the book, Highsmith plays with the idea of guilt, the emotional drain of carrying a deadly secret. Haines is consumed with guilt for what he has done, even though it cleared the way for him to accept his desired job and marry the girl of his dreams. The effect of guilt on everyday people would become a major theme in Highsmith's work. Once a character starts down the wrong path, the events and the guilt lead to the inevitable downfall as the denouement.

While most of the action revolves around Haines and Bruno with Gerard in pursuit, the women in the novel and their relationships to men are depicted in unkind terms. The unsympathetic female characters are not three-dimensional. Highsmith describes Miriam as, "On her short cheek, the sunlight picked out the largest of the freckles, and Guy saw a certain pattern he remembered and had not thought of since a time when he had been married to her. How sure he had been that he possessed her, possessed her every frailest thought! Suddenly it seemed that all love was only a tantalizing, a horrible next-best to knowing. He knew not the smallest part of the new world in Miriam's mind now. Was it possible that the same thing could happen to Anne?"[2] In Highsmith's world, the two male leads could make a bond, but the bond between man and woman was tenuous at best, a perpetual misunderstanding between the sexes.

On the other side of the coin, Highsmith was also accused of not including many women as protagonists in her books, a charge she didn't deny. "When questioned about her preference for male heroes, the author would reply: 'Women are tied to the home... Men can do more, jump over fences.'"[3] Statements like that did not endear her to feminists. Miriam is seen as manipulative and coarse. Anne is shown as a pure, sweet beauty, but she shows only vague motivations. Bruno's mother is flighty, unable to stand up to Bruno's father, and naïve about Bruno's darker nature. Women characters would not be fleshed out in Highsmith's books until much later in her career.

But if her women characters were somewhat bland, her male protagonists were shocking in comparison. Even in 1950, the idea of two men harboring a secret relationship carried a homoerotic subtext. *Strangers on a Train* is explicit about Bruno's attraction to Guy. Bruno is clearly fascinated with Guy and the book makes little pretense of hiding that desire. The film was more obtuse in its references. Bruno came off as something of a dandy in the film, but nothing overt. More homoerotic elements were retained in the British version of the film, but still both were sanitized for the general audience.

Highsmith's portrayals of same-sex attraction were some of the first in the genre. She didn't show these men as one-dimension characters; the people in her works were flesh and blood. She took great pains to bare the psyche of these relationships. Her works would be the basis for more alternative mysteries in the late 1980s and beyond. It would be almost 15 more years before George Baxt wrote of Pharaoh Love and nearly 20 before Joseph Hansen started

---

2. Patricia Highsmith. *Strangers on a Train* (New York: W.W. Norton, 1950), page 38.
3. The Guardian Unlimited, London, England, January 28, 2000

his Dave Brandstetter series.

Strangers on a Train was nominated for an Edgar in 1950 in the best first novel category, but lost to Thomas Walsh's *Nightmare In Manhattan*. Even so, Highsmith came away a winner. Hitchcock optioned the film rights for $7500. He would later declare that the final product was one of his favorite films.

In the film, Hitchcock redeemed Guy to make the movie more palatable for American audiences in the 1950s. Beyond the title and the initial premise of swapping murders, the book and novel are two very different works. In the movie, Guy is now a tennis player, wanting to marry into a Senator's family. He doesn't even consider the swapped murder and is framed by Bruno for Miriam's murder because he won't cooperate. With the help of Anne and her sister (played by Hitchcock's daughter Patricia), he is able to clear her name and bring Bruno to justice. While the final carousel scene is not in the book, it is evocative of Highsmith's vision of a world spun out of control.

Despite her newfound popularity in the suspense field, Highsmith's next work was outside the genre. She wrote a lesbian love story entitled, *The Price of Salt*. Rejected by her publisher, Highsmith published the novel under the pseudonym of Claire Morgan. The book did extremely well as one of the earliest recorded examples of a lesbian-themed novel. By most estimates, *The Price of Salt* sold over a million copies and was republished late in Highsmith's career under her own name. In 1990 when Naiad republished this book, Highsmith acknowledged it as her own work and outed herself. In the process, she became one of the earliest and most famous suspense authors to announce her sexuality.

Her following novel, *The Blunderer*, was again in the suspense field and published under her own name. In *The Blunderer*, she twists the formula she used so well in *Strangers on a Train*. "[T]he germinal idea of another book, *The Blunderer*, was not so promising, was more stubborn about developing, but showed a hardihood by sticking in my head for more than a year, and nagging at me until I found a way to write it. This was: 'Two crimes are strikingly similar, though the people who commit them do not know each other.'"[4]

As with *Strangers on a Train*, the two main characters are men, bound together by murder. In this case, one man has intentionally killed his wife, the other merely fantasized about it before his wife commits suicide. While Walter Stackhouse has not committed a crime, he has daydreamed about his wife's murder. Society punishes him for that crime by making him the outcast that his wife wanted him to be. Stackhouse is trapped in an existential nightmare, one where he is punished for the wickedness of his thoughts rather than for any deed he committed. The situation is evocative of Kafka, where no one can halt events once they have begun. The logical end is like a brick wall looming ahead. The policeman, Corby, plays the two men off each other until the situation explodes into further violence.

Again the women are not sympathetic. Clara Stackhouse, a successful businesswoman, clings to her husband with threats of suicide and promises that she will change. She is petty and neurotic, accusing her husband of starting an affair with an acquaintance before he even notices the young woman in question.

In nearly all of Highsmith's works, the plot has a point of no-return where the character could choose another direction. Once that choice is made, the inevitable path of self-destruction begins. Some critics have decried her works, saying that the suspension of disbelief is stretched too far by the extreme reactions of the characters. To Highsmith's credit, she makes the situation so plausible and real that the reader forgets that the protagonist might have avoided the entire situation. In *Strangers on a Train*, Guy could have easily not played

4. Patricia Highsmith. *Plotting and Writing Suspense Fiction*, page 4.

along with Bruno's conversation. He could have moved or read a book. In *The Blunderer*, Walter follows the bus carrying his wife to the first rest stop. His reasoning for his actions is thin, but Highsmith has so masterfully drawn the characters and situation that the reader understands the actions, even if the decisions are not what the reader would do.

In 1955, Highsmith's most celebrated work was released. *The Talented Mr. Ripley* introduces Tom Ripley to unsuspecting mystery readers. The titular character is a calculating, cold, double-murderer in just the first book alone. By the end of the series, the body count stands at eight. The first murder is a crime of passion and desire; the rest of the crimes stem from that original murder. Again, once events are set in motion, they must be played out to the final results even over multiple books if necessary.

Unlike most books at the time, not only does Tom get away with the murders, he is rewarded in the will of his victim, the ultimate irony. Tom is a man who covets the good life, and for him, this is akin to heaven. This is an ironic twist to her earlier works in which innocent men are sometimes punished for their thoughts or fantasies.

Again two men are entwined by circumstances. Tom Ripley is sent to Italy by the parents of Dickie Greenleaf to retrieve the playboy who paints and spends his time on the beach. Tom finds himself entranced by his patron's son and soon begins to emulate his behavior. The imitation irritates Dickie who wants to banish Tom back to America. Tom retaliates by killing Dickie and continuing the playboy lifestyle in Rome. The novel unfolds as Tom tries to hold the police at bay as well as the family and Marge, Dickie's quasi-girlfriend. He escapes multiple close calls to come away with the ultimate prize at the end of the book. Not surprisingly, *The Talented Mr. Ripley* won the Edgar award for best novel of the year.

Throughout her career, certain themes resonate in Highsmith's novels. Readers see the short-sighted materialism of her characters. Her characters typically search for a better life, defined by possessions. Guy is interested in "marrying up" with his second wife. In *The Talented Mr. Ripley*, Tom Ripley covets Dickie Greenleaf's social position as much as his possessions. The appearance of wealth through possessions is rampant in Ripley's life. After Ripley assumes Greenleaf's persona, he quickly sets about surrounding himself with the finer things in life. Ripley's affection for things borders on worship. "He loved to pack, and he took a long time about it, a whole day or two days, laying Dickie's clothes affectionately into suitcases, now and then trying on a good-looking shirt or a jacket in front of the mirror. He was standing in front of the mirror, buttoning a blue-and-white seahorse-patterned sport shirt of Dickie's that he had never worn, when there came a knock at his door."[5] By the time of *Ripley's Game*, he has succeeded in buying a lavish home and furnishing it with spectacular artwork and other objects that represent taste to him.

In conjunction with the materialism of her characters, Highsmith rarely uses a morally straight hero as her book's protagonist. In the Ripley series, Tom Ripley is anything but a hero. A conman, manipulator of people and events, a grifter, a sociopath perhaps, but never a romantic leading hero. He lusts for the goods of others. He punishes people according to his own set of rules. When the reader is first introduced to Ripley, he's hiding from someone he feels might be a creditor or the police.

The reader watches the events with fascination, but few people would want to emulate Tom Ripley or Guy Haines. In *Crime & Mystery: The 100 Best Books*, H.R.F. Keating recounts "I well remember a meeting of the judges for the Crime Writers' Association's Gold Dagger award where one of our number announced that if we chose *Ripley's Game* for the prize she would resign."[6] Many read-

---

5. Patricia Highsmith. *The Talented Mr. Ripley* (New York: Coward, McCann, 1955), page 139.

ers felt the same revulsion for Ripley, even though the books have been extremely popular.

Later, Highsmith would write about her creations. "I think it is also possible to make a hero-psychopath one hundred percent sick and revolting, and still make him fascinating for his very blackness and all-around depravity. I very nearly did this with Bruno in *Strangers on a Train*, for even Bruno's generosity is neither consistent nor well-placed, and there is nothing else to be said in his favor. But in that story, Bruno's evil was offset by Guy's 'goodness' which considerably simplified the problem I had of providing a likable hero, as Guy became the likable hero. It depends on the writer's skill, whether he can have a frolic with the evil in his hero-psychopath. If he can, then the book is entertaining, and in that case there is no reason why the reader should have to 'like' the hero."[7] Likewise, Dickie is less evil than Tom Ripley; Dickie's crimes are only against his family and friends, failing to live up to their expectations and wasting his fortune. By comparison, Ripley is a sociopath who wants that lifestyle, no matter what it costs to obtain it. Similarly, in *The Blunderer*, Kimmel is portrayed as a darker villain than Stackhouse who becomes a victim in the web he created.

Highsmith's protagonists are matched by a morally ambiguous counterpart, a mirror image of what the character could be. Every protagonist has an equal and opposite antagonist. In the case of the anti-hero, the reader might expect a reasonably moral opponent, but instead the alternative character is typically no better than the protagonist, just different. Tom Ripley is drawn to and covets the life of Dickie Greenleaf, who cheats on his supposed girlfriend, mooches off his parents, and wants to play at being an artist. The quasi-erotic

6. H.R.F. Keating. *Crime & Mystery: The 100 Best Books* (New York: Carol & Graf Publishers, Inc., 1987), page 113.

7. Patricia Highsmith. *Plotting and Writing Suspense Fiction*, page 47.

desire between the characters as well as the ability of Tom to switch between his own personality and that of the supposed Dickie leave the reader with two characters who combine to make one. Tom's ruthless ambition with Dickie's wealth make up the ideal capitalist. As suggested in this passage, the two nearly make a whole. "Tom darted back to the closet again and took a hat from the top shelf. It was a little grey Tyrolian hat with a green-and-white feather in the brim. He put it on rakishly. It surprised him how much he looked like Dickie with the top part of his head covered. Really it was only his darker hair that was very different from Dickie. Otherwise, his nose – or at least its general form – his narrow jaw, his eyebrows if he held them right."[8]

Highsmith was aware of her penchant for writing about the relationship of two men. In the majority of her fiction, she used some variation on this theme, whether two men exchanged murders, one man coveted the life of another or even one man who desired vengeance against another. The two main male characters were easily distinguished, especially when one was Tom Ripley. Highsmith used the contrast in the Ripley series by pitting him against a dissolute playboy, a somewhat contented married man, and even a teenaged boy. Even with Ripley's intense, intimate interactions with other men and his tepid marriage to Heloise, Highsmith always insisted that Tom was not gay, but sexually ambivalent at best.

Yet in most of the novels that have these male relationships, there is a gay-themed quality about the work. The characters in many cases do not express that desire or act upon it, but the intense emotional relationship is evocative of more. Only in the first Ripley book is there a question of sexual orientation when Ripley reassures Dickie that he is not "that way".

---

8. Patricia Highsmith. *The Talented Mr. Ripley* (New York: Coward, McCann, 1955), page 79.

While most of the characters, gay and straight, meet with horrible fates, the reader comes away with the idea that it's not because they may harbor any same-sex desires, but because of circumstances and the more universal guilt they experience. In past genre novels, characters suspected of being less than masculine were quickly relegated to supporting roles and were quickly killed off.

While Ripley was her most famous creation, he was never intended to be a series character. Twenty-five years passed before another Ripley book appeared. *Ripley Under Ground* takes place years after the first book, and Tom has established himself as a wealthy, albeit shady person of the arts. Married to Heloise, a wealthy, if vacuous, heiress, Tom lives at Belle Ombre. Unlike most of Highsmith's works, the marriage between Tom and Heloise is pleasant and frictionless. These later adventures are more concerned with threats to Ripley's insulated lifestyle than his person, reflecting Tom's obsession with material possessions. In many of these later books, Ripley and his wife do not appear in the same scenes, but the marriage, while childless, seems harmonious, if passionless.

In *Ripley Under Ground*, the threat comes from art forgeries. Tom is asked to produce the painter Derwatt to substantiate claims that Derwatt is indeed the artist of some works. Again he assumes the persona of a dead man, this time Derwatt, and murders the collector who is making inquiries. In *Ripley's Game*, Ripley manages to lure a novice, Jonathan, into murder and intrigue because the man once snubbed him at a party. While others might seethe about such an impropriety, Ripley vows revenge. When Ripley is contacted about murdering a Mafia figure, he entices Jonathan into committing the crime, and then protects both the man and himself when the Mafia come in search of revenge. Ripley kills the hired thugs who come looking for answers while Jonathan becomes increasingly fascinated by Ripley. The first-time killer is both repulsed and intrigued by Ripley, but Jonathan's wife is merely shocked that her husband could associate with a rumored criminal. As he becomes more deeply enmeshed in the killings, the rift in the marriage of Jonathan and his wife is classic Highsmith.

The Boy Who Followed Ripley shows a more paternalistic Ripley, though some critics perceived the concept of younger man/ older man love in the book. An American boy, Frank, comes to Ripley with the story that he has "accidentally" murdered his father. He thinks that Tom will understand because of the continued rumors surrounding Ripley about Dickie Greenleaf and Freddie Miles. Again Highsmith uses the concept of guilt as she portrays this young man dying inside because of what he's done.

The last book in the series was published in 1992. *Ripley Under Water* again pits Tom Ripley against a foe who wants to upset his peaceful life at Belle Ombre. An American couple moves to the same little French village. The couple knows too much about Ripley's past and proceeds to close in on him. In this final book, Ripley doesn't kill anyone, which is something of an anomaly given his history.

Highsmith would write close to 20 more novels, but none of them would match the success of her first few books. She followed *The Talented Mr. Ripley* with *Deep Water* in 1957 and then *The Two Faces of January. Deep Water* is another study of a failed marriage. Melinda Van Allen has tired of her marriage after having a baby with her husband, Vic. She takes a series of lovers, and this knowledge appalls Vic because he is afraid that word will get around about her indiscretions. Like the archetype cuckold, Vic is more concerned with his place in society more than any true heartbreak at her affairs. To scare off suitors, Vic "confesses" to Melinda's latest lover that he killed her last paramour. This admission is not true; the man had died of other causes. Still, the confession has the desired effect of ending the liaison. After he is officially exonerated of that death, Vic subsequently drowns her next lover, and then a third. Melinda and the man who might turn out to be her latest lover finally trap Vic into confessing, in much the same way that Guy Haines was caught in *Strangers on a Train*.

In 1957 Highsmith won the French *Grand Prix de Litterature Policiere* and the British Crime Writers Association awarded her a Silver Dagger in 1964. Awards like these from foreign sources only reinforced Highsmith's belief that she had been pigeonholed as a suspense writer in the U.S. and that she was under-appreciated in her birth country. In 1963, she moved permanently to Europe, where she lived and traveled in England, France and Switzerland before settling down near Berne. A number of her books were made into films by European directors with only limited release in the United States. These additional films cemented her reputation overseas.

With her move, Highsmith's novels became more global and more concerned with social issues. The claustrophobic world used with regularity during the 1950s grows wider—albeit no happier. The same inevitability leading toward disaster follows the characters.

In *The Tremor of Forgery*, Howard Ingham cannot say whether he had killed a man or even who it is that he is supposed to have killed. The novel tells the story of a screenwriter living in Tunisia in 1967, roughly during the time of Israel's Six-Day War, and Israel's drive to expand its borders. Highsmith was a proponent of Palestinian rights and argued with her publishers about dedicating a later book to their cause. Ingham decides to stay in Tunisia after he learns of his fiancée's infidelity with a film director. When Ingham wakes one night to find a man breaking into his room, he strikes the man with a typewriter. However, by morning the body and gore are cleaned up without question by the hotel staff. Ingham never discovers the identity of the man, although he suspects it to be a man named Abdullah. Ingham's lack of knowledge shows a studied indifference to the fate of Arabs by the Europeans living in the area.

In her next work, *A Dog's Ransom*, Highsmith discusses

social class and status in New York City. The Reynolds are a couple living with their dog, Lisa, a pure-bred miniature poodle. When the dog is killed by a Polish immigrant, the Pole (as he is frequently referred to in the book) leads the Reynolds to believe that the dog is alive and well. He begins to extort money from the Reynolds in exchange for the dog's return. The dog is later discovered dead and a young police officer, Clarence Duhamell, investigates the crime on his own. After growing tensions between the Pole and Duhamell, including threats against Duhamell's girlfriend, Duhamell beats the dognapper to death with his gun.

The rest of the novel pits Duhamell against his fellow police officers as they try to solve the Pole's murder. Duhamell confesses the truth to his girlfriend and to the Reynolds but denies any involvement to the police. As in earlier works, the police slowly build their case against the anti-hero as Duhamell's guilt starts to control the situation. In the end, the reader is left with doubts as to whether or not Duhamell was killed by police, but the impression is that he dies.

A Dog's Ransom is the first Highsmith work to feature a policeman as a protagonist. In the first chapters of the book, it appears that the dognapper might be the anti-hero with his disaffection for the American middle class, but after his death, the point of view changes to Duhamell who is now in opposition to the very organization he works for. In most of her novels, the police serve as the societal force punishing people for their crimes or supposed crimes. The change towards having a policeman as the main character shows the cracks in the very institutions of society. Highsmith's use of New York City lacks verisimilitude. She hadn't lived in Manhattan in over a decade and the changes to the city were not reflected. Her minorities were of Slavic extraction, not African-American , which had been growing the previous years in Manhattan. The racial tensions of the early 1960s were perhaps purposely excluded, but the novel lacks resonance because of that ommission.

In her next novel, Highsmith again looks at the disenfran-
chised. *Edith's Diary* covers Highsmith's thoughts on the place of
women in society. Edith and Brett move away from the city to the
peaceful life of the country. They live in a house with their son,
Cliffie, and Brett's father, George. In a short time, Brett finds another
woman and divorces Edith, leaving her to fend for herself with the
other two men still living with her. Although college-educated and a
writer, Edith is forced into a retail sales job where she barely makes
ends meet. *Edith's Diary* refers to the writings of the main character
who had once been a promising author. She is reduced to writing only
in her diary as she tries to support a family of men.

The dismal conditions of her life continue to drag her down.
Edith is forced to support the patriarchal structure of her life with
Brett, even after her husband's departure. George becomes progres-
sively more sick, until he is bedridden and gravely ill. Cliffie (as indi-
cated by the diminutive name) refuses to grow up and only works
part-time even though he is nearly 30. He seems sexually underdevel-
oped because of his father's infidelities. His sole sexual satisfaction
seems to come from masturbating into a sock.

A crime does occur in the book as Cliffie accidentally gives
George an overdose of pain medication, killing him. That event
serves to push Edith closer to insanity. The book ends with Edith's
death at a time when friends encourage her to seek professional assistance. The book covers 20 years of her life as she slowly loses her
grip on reality. The book is more a character study of Edith's captivity in domesticity than a suspense novel.

This type of social issues book led to more political novels
later in Highsmith's career. These latter books feature openly gay and
lesbian characters. The books pick up with the world that Highsmith
wrote about in *The Price of Salt*, but now she felt comfortable enough
to write about these topics under her own name. In *Found in the
Street*, the Sutherlands' marriage is disrupted by the wife's, Natalia's,

affair with Elsie, who is later killed by the jealous ex-girlfriend of her ex-girlfriend. Like her early works, *Found in the Street* is set in America, mostly New York City's Chelsea and Greenwich Village. The husband is accused of the crime, even though he had been remarkably accepting of the relationship. Even more than the Stack-house's marriage in *The Blunderer*, the Sutherlands go to great lengths to avoid conflict and confrontation. This avoidance technique doesn't give the reader much hope of a long-term relationship between the couple.

In *Small g: A Summer Idyll*, the title refers to a small café in Switzerland that serves a mixed clientele of gay and straight. One of the main characters is a commercial artist like (Highsmith's ferocious mother) who has lost his younger lover to a gay-bashing. The book follows the romantic peccadilloes of several of the people who frequent the café. There is almost a comedy of errors in the book as the characters try to determine each other's sexuality and romantic interests. Another death occurs, but the events are more about the relationships than guilt or crimes.

Highsmith was reluctant to share details of her private life, but kept diaries, released after her death. These documents revealed several female lovers. However, most of the diaries' romantic passages were coded, making the deciphering of the references difficult. She lived with the novelist Ann Aldrich (a pen name who is now identified as Marijane Meaker) in Bucks County, Pennsylvania in the late 1950s. That marked one of her few forays into domestic happiness.

While her personal life was less than fulfilling, Highsmith found success in a variety of forms. In addition to her success with her novels, Highsmith wrote superb short stories in the same vein as the ones she'd created in her twenties. Between 1970 and her death in 1995, Highsmith published enough short stories for seven collections and various other sales. She was incredibly prolific in these studies of human nature. While few of the stories dealt with murder, she studied the social interactions of people in the smaller form.

In "Not One of Us," Highsmith highlights the snubbing of a man with a new wife by their group of friends, leading to the outcast's suicide. The man has become so socially invisible that the cleaning woman overlooks his body for several hours and his social group doesn't hear about his death for two days. His non-existence is punctuated by the non-denominational service and the fact that the group makes up most of the wake, even though they didn't really care for the man. The group's reaction is understated, given the severity of what they have done.

In addition to the stories of alienation and death, Highsmith managed a number of themed short story anthologies as well. "Yet another departure of mine was *The Animal-Lover's Book of Beastly Murder*, thirteen short stories in which animals get the better of their masters or owners, because the latter merit comeuppance. And *My Little Tales of Misogyny* (like *The Animal-Lover's Book of Beastly Murder*, not published in the United States) consisted of seventeen very short stories on the foibles of the female sex—bitter, grim, and black-humoured. Such wanderings from the mystery-suspense genre give the writer's spirit freedom and also attract a wider variety of readers."[9]

Many of her stories were published in *Ellery Queen's Mystery Magazine* and were honored with awards and frequent anthologization. Her short story, "The Terrapin," was nominated for an Edgar in 1963. The story deals with a little boy who thinks that a turtle intended to be cooked as soup is a pet for him. Again, while the story doesn't have a mystery in it, the suspense of what will happen with the animal and the family pulls at the reader's emotions.

While Highsmith remained prolific, she slowed down in other

---

9. Patricia Highsmith. *Plotting and Writing Suspense Fiction* page 47.

ways. Her nomadic lifestyle ended. She settled in Switzerland in 1986, where she worked with an architect to build her own house there. She collected works of art in her home, including some of her own paintings. Stories abound of her odd behavior in her later years. She was known for bringing snails to restaurants and putting them on the table to keep her company while she ate alone.

Highsmith passed away in Switzerland in February of 1995, missing the resurgence of interest in her work with the high-profile release of *The Talented Mr. Ripley* in 1999, a new version of *Ripley's Game* appearing in 2003 and a collection of her short works in 2001. In all, Highsmith published twenty-some novels and seven short story collections in her lifetime.

Similar Authors Published Today:

- Dorothy Salisbury Davis
- Joan Fleming
- Michael Nava
- Laurie King's Kate Martinelli series

Bibliography

Strangers on a Train - - - - - - - - - - - - 1950
(Film: 1951, directed by Alfred Hitchcock, starring Farley
  Granger)
(Film: Once You Kiss a Stranger, 1969, directed by Robert
  Sparr, starring Paul Burke, Carol Lynley)
(Film: Throw Momma from the Train, 1989, comedic retelling
  of the original film, directed by Danny DeVito, starring Billy
  Crystal, Danny DeVito)
The Price of Salt - - - - - - - - - - - - - - 1952
(under the pen name Claire Morgan) Later reprinted as Carol
  under Highsmith's name.
The Blunderer - - - - - - - - - - - - - - - 1954
(Film: Le Meurtrier, aka Enough Rope, 1963, directed by
  Claude Autant-Lara)
The Talented Mr. Ripley - - - - - - - - - - 1955
(Film: Plein soleil, aka Purple Noon, 1960, directed by René
  Clément)
(Film: 1999, directed by Anthony Minghella, starring Matt
  Damon, Jude Law)
Deep Water - - - - - - - - - - - - - - - - 1957
(Film: Eaux profondes, aka Deep Water, 1981, directed by
  Michel Deville)
A Game for the Living - - - - - - - - - - - 1958
This Sweet Sickness - - - - - - - - - - - - 1960
(Film: Dites-lui que je l'aime, aka This Sweet Sickness, 1977,
  directed by Claude Miller, starring Gérard Depardieu)
The Cry of the Owl - - - - - - - - - - - - - 1962
(Film: Le Cri du hibou, aka The Cry of the Owl, 1986,
  directed by Claude Chabrol)
The Two Faces of January - - - - - - - - - 1964
(Film: Die Zwei Gesichter des Januar, aka The Two Faces of
  January, 1986, directed by Wolfgang Storch and Gabriela
  Zerhau)
The Glass Cell - - - - - - - - - - - - - - - 1964
Film: Die Gläserne Zelle, aka The Glass Cell, 1978, directed
  by Hans W. Geissendörfer
A Suspension of Mercy - - - - - - - - - - - 1965
*(also published as **The Story-Teller**)*

(*Film: Der Geschichtenerzähler, 1989, directed by Rainer Boldt*)
Plotting and Writing Suspense Fiction - - - 1966
Those Who Walk Away - - - - - - - - - 1967
The Tremor of Forgery - - - - - - - - - 1969
(*Film: Trip nach Tunis, 1993, directed by Peter Goedel*)
Ripley Under Ground - - - - - - - - - - 1970
(*Film: 2003, directed by John Schultz, starring Adrian Grenier*)
A Dog's Ransom - - - - - - - - - - - - - 1972
Ripley's Game - - - - - - - - - - - - - 1974
(*Film: Der Amerikanische Freund, aka The American Friend, 1977, directed by Wim Wenders, starring Dennis Hopper*)
(*Film: 2003, directed by Liliana Cavani, starring John Malkovich*)
Edith's Diary - - - - - - - - - - - - - 1977
(*Film: Ediths Tagebuch, aka Edith's Diary, 1986, directed by Hans W. Geissendörfer*)
The Boy Who Followed Ripley - - - - - - 1980
The Black House - - - - - - - - - - - - 1981
People Who Knock on the Door - - - - - 1983
Found in the Street - - - - - - - - - - - 1986
(*Film: 2001, directed by Terry Kinney*)
Ripley Under Water - - - - - - - - - - - 1991
Small g: A Summer Idyll - - - - - - - - - 1995

Short Story Collections
Eleven: Short Stories - - - - - - - - - - 1970
The Snail-Watcher and Other Stories - - - 1970
The Animal-Lover's Book of Beastly Murder 1975
Little Tales of Misogyny - - - - - - - - - 1977
Slowly, Slowly in the Wind - - - - - - - - 1979
The Black House - - - - - - - - - - - - 1981
Mermaids on the Golf Course - - - - - - 1985
Tales of Natural and Unnatural Catastrophes 1987
Nothing That Meets the Eye - - - - - - - 2002

CHAPTER 7 — Mignon G. Eberhart

Mignon Good Eberhart once described her own work as "I seat myself at the typewriter, and hope, and lurk." While her characters might be known for their lurking habits, this disingenuous description doesn't do justice to one of the best-known mystery authors of the 20th Century.

In *Crime & Mystery: The 100 Best Books*, H. R. F. Keating described Eberhart as the heir to Mary Robert Rinehart in the mystery-romance subgenre of crime fiction. She was hailed as "the American Agatha Christie." No less than Gertrude Stein described Eberhart as one of the "best mystifiers in America." Yet many critics disdain her heightened senses and heroines in jeopardy. Her specialty has now been largely ceded to romance fiction's suspense category.

Born in Lincoln, Nebraska, Mignon Good studied at Nebraska Wesleyan University from 1917 to 1920, leaving without a degree from the university. However, in 1935, when her rising fame became apparent, the university awarded her an honorary Doctorate of Literature.

In 1923 she married Alanson C. Eberhart, a civil engineer. The couple spent their first years in the Midwest. Alanson traveled frequently for his work, and Mignon accompanied him, finding herself alone in small towns with nothing to do. She began writing short stories to escape the boredom of traveling. After working as a freelance journalist, she decided to become a full-time fiction writer.

When her short stories stopped selling, she turned to novels; her first, *The Patient in Room 18*, was published in 1929. The novel featured nurse Sarah Keate, who assisted police detective, Lance O'Leary. The crime-solving pair would meet in four more novels in the early thirties before Eberhart turned to writing non-series romantic suspense. Sarah also appeared without O'Leary in two much later novels.

The couple made an intriguing detective team. Their pairing happened more by fate than by scheme. They never appeared on the scene at the request of the other. The younger policeman and the older nurse didn't succumb to romance, although Keate expresses an interest, and O'Leary holds a certain amused affection for the bold nurse. Eberhart once said of the redoubtable, red-haired Nurse Keate, "I loved her because she had a good sharp tongue." The dry sarcastic wit of Keate came directly from the author who was reported to have a sardonic, understated sense of humor herself.

The second of the Keate/O'Leary novels, *While the Patient Slept*, garnered the $5,000 Doubleday Doran Scotland Yard Prize in 1931. The prize established Eberhart's career as a writer. Along with a series of movies about the detective pair, the award brought national recognition to Eberhart.

Both *The Patient in Room 18* and *While the Patient Slept* are traditional mystery novels. The first book takes place in a provincial hospital and provides a variation on the locked-room mystery. The patient in Room 18 is receiving cancer treatments and is murdered to enable a thief to escape with valuable medicinal radium. The book is atmospheric and Eberhart uses the eerie night shift in the hospital to great effect. O'Leary solves the crime and confronts the various suspects in a surprise ending similar to other Golden Age narratives.

Eberhart's second outing, *While the Patient Slept*, provides a twist on the country home mystery when Sarah Keate is called in to take care of a wealthy stroke victim. At first, the job seems simple as she is only asked to watch a comatose man, but she finds secrets and schemes before she even sets foot in the Federie mansion. A vicious watchdog guarding the house establishes a fixed number of suspects. While various family members and hangers-on gather in the patient's gothic mansion to await his recovery, a series of murders take place, once again requiring the investigative talents of O'Leary. With Keate's help, the detective sorts out the suspects. In another dramatic confrontation scene, O'Leary reveals the murderer and explains the crime. Both of these early novels show Eberhart in the beginning stages of her career, working with the elements that she would perfect in her later novels.

While the Patient Slept begins with Sarah Keate bossing around a hapless taxi driver who crashes the cab after a poke from her umbrella. The humor stemming from Keate is a pleasant addition to these first few books. Keate's subsequent walk to Federie mansion reveals the odd house and gardens as well as clues in the form of overheard conversation, a hallmark of Eberhart's stories.

The setting in *While the Patient Slept* is a dreary mansion requiring lamps and candles because of the owner's refusal to get electricity. Eberhart highlights the difference between place and characters by contrasting the gothic mansion with the colors and fashion of the people as well as the color and texture of the possessions. The characters are costumed in brightly colored beads and jewelry. Even the policeman, O'Leary, is described as something of a dandy. The main clue, a carved jade green elephant statue, reflects the disparity between the bleak surroundings and the home's contents.

The book was made into a movie, the first of Eberhart's works to be released on film. The movie was faithful to the book, keeping the characters, plot and setting of the novel. The film adds a certain amount of humorous interplay between Keate and O'Leary, which is more implied than explicit in the books. O'Leary was aged in the movie; apparently, flirtation could not exist between an older nurse and younger police detective. The film was part of a series of an O'Leary / Keate series that would establish Eberhart's reputation as a premier mystery author.

The next Keate / O'Leary novel, *The Mystery of Hunting's End*, published in 1930, shows Eberhart's use of landscape and architecture in her work. The action in the book is set in the Sand Hills of Nebraska, not far from where Eberhart grew up. The driving snow that traps the group into the hunting lodge becomes a constant factor in the book.

The book features Sarah Keate and Lance O'Leary in another locked room mystery. The house map is important to the story and is graphically represented in the book. Despite the fact that her last novel was another variation on the country house murder, Eberhart was not above repeating similar plot elements in subsequent books. This sometimes led to complaints about a lack of originality in her work.

In typical fashion, the pair are thrown together, rather than working in tandem to solve the case. Keate is caring for an invalid aunt of the hostess while O'Leary has been invited to look into a past murder. Matil Kingery invites the same set of people to the hunting lodge who stayed there five years ago when her father was murdered. She decides to revisit the murder at this time because she has fallen in love with one of the suspects.

Yet Matil refuses to tell O'Leary and Keate who her beau is. The duality of the mystery means that the romance is played for the same stakes as the criminal activities. This seems to be a common thread in many of Eberhart's books, putting the romance on the same level of intensity as the fatal crime. The book moves rather slowly until the murder and is at its best during the convoluted explanation of the locked room solution.

Eberhart's next book, *From the Dark Stairway*, was again set in a hospital during the night shift. The setting is reminiscent of *The Patient in Room 18*, but this time the doctor is murdered. Keate has been brought in to nurse a rich patient, Peter Melady, who is suffering from heart trouble. Just prior to surgery, the doctor attending Melady is found dead in the elevator and Peter Melady is missing, despite his precarious health.

The police and Keate search for Melady's missing formula for an anesthetic, which will replace ether, worth millions of dollars. By convenience, Melady's daughter and the doctor's wife are both patients in the hospital at the same time, along with the doctor's first wife. Hospital security provides a finite number of suspects, and Eberhart makes good use of the least likely suspect to come up with the solution.

These early works show Eberhart's ties to the gothic mystery. This tradition of mystery traces its roots back to 1846 and *Jane Eyre*. With its long-suffering narrator, and the moody Mr. Rochester with his many secrets, the book inspired an entire movement of gothic novels. The mystery elements of the woman in the attic and the deeply atmospheric settings created the hallmarks for an entirely new subgenre of fiction. In the early part of the twentieth century, Mary Roberts Rinehart stood as the premier author of the form; Eberhart was hailed as the successor to Rinehart's work. Because of the form's popularity, it generated a large number of imitators and the books' quality declined. Detractors criticized large plot holes where the heroine makes the nearly fatal error of investigating the attic without telling a soul or traipsing through the empty mansion at night with no means of defense. The feeling was that the loss of common sense was merely an overused gimmick to further a thin plot.

In the first several of Eberhart's books, the heroine is a trained nurse, who should be aware of the risks involved in impetuous behavior. Yet Sarah Keate often scuttles down a dark hallway in the middle of the night without any protection. In *From the Dark Stairway*, Keate goes into a darkened room despite the knowledge that the killer is after her.

Eberhart also led the way with the nurse heroine, a device used by many other authors of the time. For some time, it looked as though most of Eberhart's works would be set around hospitals. The nurse was an ideal character to be both female and in peril. Keate was one of the better examples of this. Eberhart used a hospital setting in several of her books, and made good use of the hospital routine to create her mysterious happenings.

Another hallmark of gothic work is the attention to atmosphere and its description. Darkness, fog, haze, and rainstorms veil the events of the book. The atmosphere is heightened in some of Eberhart's descriptive passages. In *The Dark Garden*, the heroine finds herself driving in sleet, ice and fog outside Chicago. The driver describes the scene in minute detail because of the difficulty in driving in those weather conditions. The descriptions can deal with the perceptions of the heroine as well. The heroine of a story brings supernormal senses that border on the hallucinatory. She can hear the sounds of humming or footsteps in the hallway. In *The Dark Garden*, she writes:

> "Charlotte Weinberg sat listening.
> There was, she realized, nothing to hear.
> The whole great house was silent. Had there been any sound, particularly any stealthy, unaccustomed sound, she would have heard it at once. The room in which she was sitting was the very hub and center of the house. Into it opened the wide front entrance with only an open vestibule intervening, and from it on the opposite side opened the door leading out upon a strip of lawn ending in a white railing, broken where beach steps went downward out of sight, and then gray lake and gray sky.
> And from that room branched like a tree all the other sections of the house, the main stem of which was the wide carpeted walnut stairway, which turned over a small coatroom on its somber way to the two upper floors.
> Charlotte sat with her narrow back stiffly erect in one of the shiny black wicker chairs which, with the array of ferns which lined the windows, did not look gay and frivolous as they were intended to look, but, instead, faintly funereal. On sunny days the wide windows brought the dancing blue of the lake and sky almost into the room, but on dark days, like that day, there

was nothing gay in the room. The windows let you see, through spikes of green ferns, a strip of wet, brownish lawn and at its end a railing and then just gray space as if the world had dropped away there beyond the railing.

It was, thought Charlotte with irritation, a typical February fog that was creeping inexorably up from the lake. Presently it would sift through tightly closed windows and doors and would crawl silently through the house and would tickle her long, sensitive throat, and she would cough and Mina, upstairs, would grow nervous."[1]

The form earned numerous critics after the war and into the 1950s; the term "gothic" became pejorative. The antipathy to the sub-genre grew with the naming of the form as the "Had I But Known" school, for the tendency of the heroines to get into mortal danger after uttering "had I but known what lay in wait for me upstairs." Ridicule only hastened its demise. Unfortunately, the HIBK style has gone out of vogue at the current time, but a number of authors converted the subgenre to a more generic romantic suspense form, which can be found in many romance sections. Many publishing houses have a romantic suspense imprint; no less than Nora Roberts writes mysteries under the pen name of "J.D. Robb."

While most of Eberhart's works are in the same vein, she by no means limited herself to novel length works. Before her novels were published, she dabbled in the short form and wrote novelettes as well. Her ear for dialog also gave her an opening into drama. Her stage play, *320 College Avenue*, was written with Fred Ballard, and *Eight O'Clock Tuesday* written with Robert Wallsten ran on Broadway for two weeks in 1941. Her efforts also stretched into teaching other authors as part of the Famous Writers School.

Her multi-faceted skills provided her with a comfortable life-

---

1. Mignon G. Eberhart. *The Dark Garden*, Random House (New York, 1933),

style. Sales of all her works provided Eberhart with a good income. By 1935, she was one of the top female authors of the era, earning no less than $35,000 a year. She found the serialization market to be quite profitable along with her consistent marketing efforts to publicize her works.

In 1934, Eberhart compiled a collection of short stories about a mystery writer who dabbles in murder. In many ways, that collection, *The Cases of Susan Dare*, marked a delineation in Eberhart's career. She was finished with more traditional mysteries and the idea of a mystery series. This collection of short stories (which originally appeared in *The Delineator*) features traditional mysteries, and a pairing with an ambitious newspaper reporter. This would be the only collection featuring mystery author Susan Dare.

Eberhart's books after this point would be standalone works. Young beautiful heroines, typically dependent on others for money and financial security, would replace the feisty Sarah Keate. Eberhart's trademark would become the non-series novel, which offered a well-judged blend of exotic locales, wealthy characters, atmospheric suspense, and romance seen through the eyes of a sympathetic female heroine. Almost all of her works were written in the first person singular from the view of a woman, not always one who is young and gorgeous. Her best works combine these elements with a strong sense of place, one where the description become almost palatable. The books frequently contain an element of the supernatural or the suspected supernatural as the heroine can think of no means for the occurrence other than the paranormal.

While well known for her deeply atmospheric descriptions, Eberhart concentrated on the characters in her work. In a letter to a student at the Famous Writers School, she explained, "any writer thinks and thinks and thinks about his characters and his story. I like to put the thinking as much as I can on paper, before I start the story. Then I like to simmer the long notes down, so to speak, until I have only the essential facets. I then have something specific, something written down on paper, a kind of framework or an entrance to the story; this is a help to me. I find that in the process I have become thoroughly acquainted with the characters so I am more likely to know what they will say or do."[2]

Eberhart jumped into this new choice of form by writing one and sometimes two books a year. In less than seven years, she'd produced nine novels and a short story collection. She followed *The Dark Garden* with *The White Cockatoo*, *The House on the Roof*, and *Fair Warning*.

Fair Warning proved that Eberhart could twist her own genre. She bristled at the term "Gothic" writer, but fans recognized the traits in Eberhart's works. In *Fair Warning*, she took several of the gothic novel's conventions and used the expectations to surprise the reader. The book opens with the return of Ivan Godden after a month's stay in the hospital following an automobile accident. Marcia Godden is married to a sadistic man who abuses her in a million subtle ways. When Ivan is murdered, she becomes the prime suspect and the earlier car accident is subject to scrutiny as well. The love letters between Marcia and the next-door neighbor, Rob Copley, disappear and become the property of the police through an anonymous source. When Beatrice, Ivan's sister, is murdered by identical means, the noose tightens around Marcia's neck. She must carefully look at the people around her to determine who is the murderer. While the book contains the usual lurking in the dark and sounds in the night, the book stands some gothic conventions on their ears, leaving a relatively straightforward murder mystery. To Eberhart's credit, the reader doesn't discover the reversed expectations until the end of the book.

Her next novel, *Danger in the Dark*, went back to Eberhart's more formulaic plots and one of her more popular plot devices, the wedding in jeopardy. In *Danger in the Dark*, Daphne Haviland has arranged to marry Ben Brewer, the president of the Haviland Bridge Company, which her grandfather founded and left for Ben to operate. In order to protect the estate and the family's fortune, she is pushed into a loveless union with Brewer despite her deep feelings for her dis-

---

2. Letter from Mignon Eberhart to Gordon Caroll (in association with the fame writers program/school), from 1960, part of the Eberhart collection at Boston University.

tant cousin, Dennis. Ben is found murdered on the bride's estate just hours before the nuptials. Because they had a secret rendezvous in the springhouse, Daphne and Dennis are considered suspects in the murder. However, the entire family is beholden to Brewer for their financial future, so everyone at the Haviland estate had a motive. Despite the mysterious departure of a woman from the estate minutes before Ben was found murdered, the discovery of a bridal bouquet flower makes it appear as if one of the family is guilty. Dennis and Daphne are forced to solve the crime, clear their own names, and resolve the matters of the family business before they can marry at the end of the book.

Her next book, *Hasty Wedding*, reversed the same wedding formula. The boyfriend is murdered and the wedding takes place. Dorcas Whipple has come home to Chicago after a romantic interlude with Ronald Drew in Florida. Upon return, her plans include marrying a family friend, Jevan Locke. When Ronald contacts Dorcas in Chicago they arrange a meeting. Ronald threatens to kidnap her and vows that he would rather kill himself than see her marry another man. When Ronald is found dead the next morning, Jevan rushes through the wedding while Dorcas is still in a state of shock. While the act seems heartless at first, Dorcas discovers that Ronald was murdered and Jevan married her because he knows that she was with the victim just before his death. Marriage means that Jevan cannot testify against his wife, who he thinks killed Ronald. By the book's end, Dorcas and Jevan have realized that despite the forced circumstances of their marriage that they are truly in love. This was the only one of the non-Keate books to be filmed.

In her next book, *The Hangman's Whip*, Eberhart took a break from the interrupted wedding scenarios, but resumed with the plot of the young couple kept apart by a spouse who won't stand aside. After a long separation, Search Abbott and Howland Stacy meet again. Search's Aunt Ludmilla requests her presence at the estate because the elderly woman thinks that someone is trying to poison her. Ludmilla only trusts Search, who has not been present at the time of the poisonings. When Search returns to the estate, she meets up with Howie who had hastily married Eve a few years before. He tells Search that it's over between Eve and him and that he has always cared more for Search. Before they can act on this declaration, Eve returns to the estate and is murdered. Search believes that the plot to poison Ludmilla is somehow tied to Eve's murder. Since Eve had decided to stay married to Howie, both Search and the recent widower are accused of the crimes. The couple grows close as they try to prove their innocence so they can marry.

Eberhart returned to her interrupted marriage formula with the next book, *With This Ring*. The book opens with the recently married Rony Chatonier visiting the plantation in New Orleans of her sick husband, Eric. The family is cold to her especially after Eric announces that he is leaving his entire estate to Rony. When the body of a family friend is discovered on a small boat at the estate's dock, Rony finds a note in the dead man's hand accusing her of murder. Before she can contact the police the best man from the wedding, Stuart Westover, appears on the scene. The pair bond in trying to extricate Rony from being arrested for murder. Eric is killed, leaving Rony free to pursue a relationship with Stuart. It also leaves her vulnerable to charges that she killed both men.

Rony is one of Eberhart's most exasperating heroines. Characters like her were partly responsible for Eberhart's reputation in the "Had I But Known" category. Rony discovers the body of Judge Henry after going to the yacht by herself after dark, yet the discovery doesn't quell her need to put herself into unnecessary danger. Rony continually tromps around the estate in the middle of the night and actually goes out in the boat on a foggy night to meet the suspected killer. A dark and windy night that could cover the sound of screams is not the night to be out alone. Fortunately, Stuart saves Rony, but heroines who defy all logic became more prevalent as Eberhart wrote more books. Her publisher became increasingly sensitive to the subject and frequently corresponded with the author to provide better motivation for the characters to go in search of danger.

The Man Next Door moves towards some of the hallmarks that would typify Eberhart's later books: the young secretary in love with the boss, the mysterious death that points to the object of the heroine's affection, and glamorous settings. Maida Lovell has moved to Washington, DC, following her boss Steve Blake to an important government position. She is in love with Steve, but he seems intent on squiring Washington women around town. When Steve's gun and boutonniere are found next to the body of one of Steve's romantic rivals, an unscrupulous man begins to blackmail Maida into providing government secrets in exchange for not revealing what the man knows about the murder. By the book's end, Steve professes his love for Maida and she has been valiantly rescued from the spies. Even so, the plotting is weaker since most readers of the time felt that talking to Steve would have been preferable to betraying thousands of men on Army transports and endangering their lives for love.

Even though Eberhart dedicated *Hasty Wedding* in 1939 to her husband Alan "who still listens," Eberhart's own love life proved as tumultuous as her character's romances. Her long marriage to Eberhart deteriorated during the war years. She divorced Alanson Eberhart for John Hazen Perry who she hastily married in 1946. The new union was not a happy one. She realized her error too late, but two years later she divorced Perry and remarried her first husband.

Eberhart's post-war efforts marked an improvement from her war year books. In *Another Woman's House*, Eberhart brought back the country manor murder and a true mystery to be solved. Eberhart evokes the same claustrophobic tension of *Rebecca*. Myra Lane is the young ward of Lady Carmichael. Both women go to live with Richard Thorne after Richard's wife, Alice, is convicted of murdering her lover. Richard announces his love to Myra, but before they can marry, Alice is cleared of the crimes by a confession of perjury by the lone eyewitness. Richard is in love with Myra, but plagued with guilt about not believing his wife and thinking that Alice had been unfaithful to him prior to the murder. With the reopening of the criminal case, the killings begin almost immediately.

In *Dead Men's Plans*, a family is torn apart when Reg Minary brings home a strange woman as his wife. The woman shares a past with more than one person in the family and she quickly tries to take control of the family business. Sewal Blake is the stepsister to the Minary children and engaged to the current president of the company, much like Eberhart's earlier work, *Danger in the Dark*. Sewal's true love, Barny, returns and Sewal finds herself in trouble as a killer decides to alter the family business' organization chart.

In many of her later works, Eberhart uses the post-war diaspora to engineer her couples. She frequently wrote about groups of children who had grown up together and who had paired off in early adulthood. With the war and all the changes that happened after it, the groups separated, only to meet up later and realize that the earlier relationship was the one that was meant to be. The early couplings, like the one in Eberhart's life, were the ones that endured, not the quick affair that seemed to rend these couples apart. However, many times the couples who were split up by time and events are afraid that they are only perceived as friends and nothing more.

With *The Unknown Quantity*, Eberhart again goes back to the idea of the government plot with a husband who found murdered while serving his country. His last request to his wife and a mysterious stranger who bears an uncanny resemblance to the husband, was to pretend to be man and wife for one week to throw off any enemy spies who might be keeping tabs on the man. The husband is killed, and the couple is put in danger as they wonder if they can trust each other while trying not to be the next victims of the unknown killers.

Sarah Keate returned in *Man Missing*, Eberhart's next effort. Despite the passage of nearly 30 chronological years, Keate seems only a few years older than her last case from the 1930s. The new Keate book reminded readers of how far Eberhart's work had come from those original detective tales set in the early 1930s. In this book, Keate is serving as a nurse on a Naval Base in the middle of the desert. Much like the earlier cases, the geography of the case creates a small number of people who could have committed the crime. She discovers a dead man in the hospital where she works, evoking her earlier cases like *The Patient in Room 18* and *From the Dark Stairway*. Keate sees the stripes of an officer leaving the hospital minutes before the murder is discovered and the base must look for a killer among its own elite.

It's a nice change to have the narrator as the sharp-tongue Keate who is more self-reliant and observant than most of the latter day Eberhart heroines.

In *Another Man's Murder*, Eberhart goes back to her familiar plotline. Cayce Clary returns home to Florida and his orange groves at the request of his uncle, the Judge. Cayce and the old man argue and Cayce heads back to his home in New York. He decides to stay at the last minute and deplanes to find the police waiting for him in connection with his uncle's murder.

The plotline is convoluted and somewhat preposterous. The characters in this book seem to dance more to the tune of the plot rather than breathe as people on the page. Cayce and Dodie Howard, the next door neighbor, had eloped prior to the beginning of the book and they never bothered to see if the judge had truly annulled the marriage or not. The couple then decides to stay married. The deed to the house is never recorded, and the clauses in the father's will are most unusual and not reported to anyone.

In 1965, after thirty plus years of writing, Eberhart proved that she still had a flair for writing. Her work that year was *R.S.V.P. Murder*, later selected as one of the best 100 crime and mystery books by H.R.F. Keating, not because it was far and away the best of her works, but because it was indicative of the best elements of her other works. "In many ways it shows M.G. Eberhart at her most typical." Keating cites the exotic locale of the book, taking place on the French Riviera. The rich and socially elite milieu make up the story characters, something that Keating calls a requirement for Eberhart's books. Then there is the heightened atmosphere, where suspense is brought to a crescendo through hints and telltale word choices.

In *R.S.V.P. Murder*, Fran, a young penniless orphan learns that her father is not the man she thought he was. Just before his death, the late lawyer sent out a series of letters to his clients who possessed secrets, informing them that they must provide support for his daughter. When her life is endangered, Fran decides to track down each of the five letters and to find out what the secrets were. However, she has no idea to whom the blackmail letters were sent. Of course, in the process of tracking down the clients and making things right, she falls in love.

In *Message from Hong Kong*, Marcia Lowry decides to track down her missing husband, Dino, when a small piece of jade is sent to the family home wrapped in newspaper bearing the name of a man in Hong Kong. When she arrives in Hong Kong, she learns that the man she is seeking died years ago. The current proprietor of the shop that sold the jade piece is murdered before Marcia can get any answers from him. However, she does receive an odd list of names, cities and numbers from the proprietor. While being questioned by the police, she is joined by her intended, Richard, who wants Marcia to declare Dino dead so that she can marry him. Marcia and Richard circumnavigate the globe in order to find out what the names and numbers represent and learn who had killed the proprietor and the fate of her long-missing husband.

Just the sheer volume of her work made Eberhart a name to be reckoned with. From the beginning of her career, Eberhart seemed to write at a prodigious pace. She wrote a novel nearly every year, producing almost 60 novels before her death. In 1971 she garnered the Grand Master award from the Mystery Writers of America. Eberhart was only the second woman mystery writer (after Agatha Christie) to receive the prestigious award. She published her 59th and final novel, *Three Days for Emeralds* (1988), shortly before her 89th birthday. Her increasing age made writing difficult.

In 1994, she was awarded the Malice Domestic Lifetime Achievement award for her contributions to the mystery field. She died in Greenwich, Connecticut, on October 8, 1996.

Similar Authors Published Today:

- Phyllis Whitney
- Elizabeth Peters/Barbara Michaels
- Mary Higgins Clark
- Nora Roberts/J.D. Robb
- Lillian Stewart Carl
- Anne Stuart
- Eileen Dreyer

Bibliography

The Patient in Room 18 - - - - - - - - - - 1929
*(Film: 1938, directed by Bobby Connolly and Crane Wilburm
starring Ann Sheridan)*
While the Patient Slept - - - - - - - - - - 1930
*(Film: 1935, directed by Ray Enright, starring Aline MacMa-
hon)*
The Mystery of Hunting's End - - - - - - - 1930
*(Film: Mystery House, 1938, directed by Noel M. Smith, star-
ring Ann Sheridan and Dick Purcell)*
From the Dark Stairway - - - - - - - - - - 1931
*(Film: The Murder of Dr. Harrigan, 1936, directed by Frank
McDonald)*
*(Film: The Dark Stairway, 1938, directed by Arthur B. Woods,
starring Hugh Williams)*
Murder by an Aristocrat - - - - - - - - - - 1932
(UK title: Murder of My Patient)
(Film: 1936, directed by Frank McDonald)
The Dark Garden - - - - - - - - - - - - - 1933
(UK title: Death in the Fog)
The White Cockatoo - - - - - - - - - - - - 1933
(Film: 1935, directed by Alan Crosland, starring Jean Muir)
The House on the Roof - - - - - - - - - - - 1935
Fair Warning - - - - - - - - - - - - - - - 1936
Danger in the Dark - - - - - - - - - - - - 1937
(UK title: Hand in Glove)
The Pattern - - - - - - - - - - - - - - - - 1937
(UK title: Pattern of Murder)
The Glass Slipper - - - - - - - - - - - - - 1938
Hasty Wedding - - - - - - - - - - - - - - 1938
*(Film: Three's a Crowd, 1945, directed by Lesley Selander,
starring Pamela Blake)*
Brief Return - - - - - - - - - - - - - - - 1939
The Chiffon Scarf - - - - - - - - - - - - - 1939
The Hangman's Whip - - - - - - - - - - - 1940
Speak No Evil - - - - - - - - - - - - - - - 1941
With This Ring - - - - - - - - - - - - - - 1941
Wolf in Man's Clothing - - - - - - - - - - 1942
The Man Next Door - - - - - - - - - - - - 1943

Short Story Collections

The Cases of Susan Dare - - - - - - - - - -	1934
Five of My Best - - - - - - - - - - - - - -	1949
Deadly is the Diamond - - - - - - - - - - -	1951
Deadly is the Diamond and	
Three Other Novelettes of Murder - - - -	1958
The Crimson Paw - - - - - - - - - - - - -	1959
Mignon G. Eberhart's Best Mystery Stories	1988

Index

Atomic Renaissance

DISCARD